TAROT CARD MEANINGS

An Apprentice Guide of General Interpretations
of an Upright Tarot Card in a Reading
for Love, Career, and Other Matters

KEVIN HUNTER

WARRIOR
OF LIGHT
PRESS
Los Angeles, California

The author of this book does not dispense medical advice or prescribe the use of any technique as a form of treatment for physical, emotional, or medical problems without the advice of a physician, either directly or indirectly. The intent of the author is only to offer information of a general nature to help you in your quest for emotional and spiritual well-being. In the event, you use any of the information in this book for yourself, which is your constitutional right, the author and the publisher assume no responsibility for your actions.

Warrior of Light Press
www.kevin-hunter.com

Religion & Spirituality/Divination/Tarot
Body, Mind & Spirit/New Thought
Inspiration & Personal Growth

DEDICATION

This is for the apprentice Tarot user
on your reading journey.

CONTENTS

THE CARDS

Major Arcana

Minor Arcana

The Wands/Fire Suit

The Swords/Air Suit

The Pentacles/Earth Suit

The Cups/Water Suit

INTRODUCTION

*T*he various meanings of each Tarot card listed in this book were tested on an audience of novices for feedback and input to ensure its comprehendible. The idea to write the *Tarot Card Meanings* sat around for several years in development. My initial reason for doing this had purely selfish motives behind it. I thought it would be fun to take the Tarot journey alone and break it out talking only about what the meaning could be in a reading.

I've received notes from people over the years about a card they pulled not knowing what the messages could be in response to their question. Many had read my interpretations of the different cards and a demand rose asking for more like it. I realized that there were others who were interested in this too! I decided to do this for myself and then release it in book form for my readers who were interested.

There is a great deal of information out there on the Tarot, but many novices that approached me found it to be vague, challenging, or incomprehensible leaving them even more confused. All they wanted to know was basic day-to-day concerns, such as whether or not a potential date would be the long term relationship person, or if they should quit their job and find a new one. Love and career are two of the biggest topics I am asked about more than any other subject. Therefore, I decided to focus on the general essence meanings of each Tarot card with a heavy up on love and career. I hope what is in this book can assist you along on your Tarot journey, but in the end it is up to you as the reader to come to your judgements and conclusions as to what the Tarot is telling you.

In the potential meanings for each card I may interchange the pronouns *he* or *she* because that's more efficient than saying *he/she*. Please replace it with the pronoun that is most comfortable for you.

~ Kevin Hunter

Tarot Card Meanings

Connecting with a
Tarot Card

⚜

I've been a Tarot enthusiast user since I was a child. I was eight years old staring at the dynamically stimulating images of the cards, and allowing all of the elements surrounding them to hit me like a tsunami wave. This is the same way I would sift through my parent's record collection fixating on the album covers when vinyl was the big thing. The images of the album covers were as vibrant and layered with detail as a Tarot card.

There are endless messages that can come through from staring at any image, let alone a Tarot card. If you have an attraction to art or a painting, and find yourself picking up on what's unsaid and getting lost in the caverns of it, then you're that much closer to being able to efficiently and adequately reading a Tarot card.

I've met CEO's who won't make a decision without connecting with the Tarot. Anyone can consult with the cards regardless of what position you hold in life. It doesn't matter if you're a lawyer, doctor, surfer, receptionist, garbage man, plumber, or politician. The Tarot is an exceptional communication device to receive messages, wisdom, and guidance from your Spirit team for any human soul on the planet.

The brilliance of the Tarot is that it's for anyone who has a passion for the cards. There are endless varying takes of the meanings of Tarot cards in a reading that one tried or true way doesn't exist.

When you feel confident enough with the cards, then you'll have your own methods that work.

I've always found the Tarot to be an excellent divination tool from which to confirm messages with my own Spirit team whenever I felt the incoming messages to be hazy or unclear. Spirit would then guide me to the right Tarot card to flip over so I could see or confirm what they wanted me to know through a card. Spirit communicates through symbols and signs as well as other means that can get your attention. Since the Tarot is ripe with symbolism, this is a great way for them to relay particular messages to you.

Diving into the worlds of the Tarot can take a lifetime of endless study. When you enjoy what you're immersing yourself into, then it ends up being a gratifying experience.

How I Connect with the Tarot

My Spirit team has been communicating with me through my etheric *clair* channels throughout the course of my entire life. Everyone has this ability since these etheric channels reside within all souls. The unseen senses are one of the many ways that Spirit can communicate with you. My soul, mind, and body has been an extraordinary vessel of psychic communication without the use of any other device.

This is a physical world with an enormous coating of thick density that acts as a wall between this world and the next. Earthly distractions, erratic emotions, and physical pleasures can block or dim the communication line with Spirit. There might be moments when your vibration is not as high as it could be. The Divine messages coming through are not loud enough, or your ego steps in to second guess what's relayed. This is where the Tarot or any Oracle for that matter can be of benefit.

The Tarot is an extension of myself when seeking to expand or confirm what's coming through. I throw down a card and flip it over only to find that the message is the one my Spirit team had informed me about. I use the Tarot partially to confirm information I'm picking up on and because it's fun to play with. It's like someone who loves playing Blackjack or any other fun card games. I find the Tarot equally enjoyable and entertaining. It is also a way for me to have a phone call with my Spirit team on the other side when the supplementary ways they communicate are not coming in clear enough. This is no different than what anyone can do when you tune in to everything that is outside of the physical concrete world that distracts you.

How You Can Connect with the Tarot

All souls are born with etheric gifts of communication that vary from one person to the next. There are four primary clairs *(clear)* called Clairvoyance *(clear seeing)*, Clairsentience *(clear feeling)*, Clairaudience *(clear hearing)*, and Claircognizance *(clear knowing)*.

Everyone has one or two dominate clairs as the primary means of communicating with Spirit.

Clairaudience and Claircognizance have been my dominate clear channels with my Spirit team since birth. This is followed by strong degrees of Clairsentience and a good measure of Clairvoyance. These are some of the channels I use to communicate with my Spirit team. The way I communicate with Spirit isn't any different than what every soul on the planet is capable of when they tune in to their extra sensory perception and all that is beyond the physical world distractions. Heaven is communicating with you through your *clair* channels as well as through signs, symbols, numbers, and the various divination tools that exist such as the Tarot.

Claircognizance: Some may know the answers without knowing how they know them. It filters in through their consciousness from above. Clairvoyance: Others may see the messages and guidance playing for them like a mini-movie through their third eye. Clairsentience: There are those who feel the answers coming to them with a thick heavy feeling sense that alerts them to a warning of danger, or an uplifting sense that something amazing is about to happen. Clairaudience: There are those who can hear the messages being spoken as if someone is in the room with them.

Every soul on the planet picks up on psychic information

regardless if they believe in a higher power or not. It is present and at their disposal. If someone is not aware of this Heavenly connection, then they are experiencing what is called a block. There are many souls who are not in tune to the vibrations from beyond, and the communication line is non-existent within them. They can awaken their spiritual sight by doing the work it takes to make that happen.

Every soul on the planet also has one Spirit Guide and one Guardian Angel that assists you along your Earthly journey here. They are what makes up your Spirit team. If someone has been working with Heaven (*a.k.a. the Other Side, Spirit World*) regularly, or has large life purposes that need extra support, then they may have more than one guide and angel around them.

Your Spirit team is communicating with you daily whether you are aware of it or not. They will communicate with you through one or more of your *clair* channels. Pay attention to your *clair* senses in order to pick up on the messages and guidance filtering through you from God, a higher power, your higher self, universe, heaven, your guides, angels, or whoever you're comfortable with calling it. In the end, the messages and guidance are coming in from beyond the physical materialistic distracting world known as the Earthly life.

Having crystal clear communication with your Spirit team can assist you with your Tarot readings. Tarot is a great divination tool to help you in picking up on what is being relayed. This is especially helpful if your clair channels have dimmed, you're second guessing the guidance, or you feel you're not picking up on anything.

Reading for Yourself and Others

I've been reading with hundreds and hundreds of people since I was a teenager as I enjoy the psychic craft. I've unsurprisingly also made many friends in the process. Every single reader reads differently from one another. There are no two people who read exactly the same way. This is because everyone has varying gifts in the way they interpret messages from the other side. If one reader doesn't work for you, then there will be a reader who does. This also means that you likely read and interpret differently than others do.

It is often advised that you avoid reading for yourself. This is because you may unknowingly taint your reading by bending it to suit what you're desiring. This won't stop anyone from reading for themselves, but take precaution by being as objective as possible when you do.

Avoid reading for yourself or for anyone when you're not in a state of psychic reception. This means if you're emotionally upset, angry, depressed, or any other negative emotion, then this can fault the reading. The same goes if you're doing a reading while on a drug chemical high, wasted on alcohol, or if you've consumed a large meal or toxic foods. This can make the reading come off all over the place and unclear.

Many professional psychics avoid reading for those close to them because they're not emotionally objective enough to give their best friend a clear reading. They will be gentler with the reading and attempt to read in a way that benefits the friend. Once you do that, then you've begun the process of contaminating the reading. The clearest readings are when the reader is centered, operating from a high vibration, focused, objective, and emotionally detached from the client.

It's common to read for oneself and bend the read to fit the answer you're hoping for. I've watched novices pull one card after another because they were unhappy with the card they were originally given. Once you do that, you've corrupted the read and created a false reading that will not be based in truth.

One is not always objective with their own stuff and requires someone who is emotionally detached from themselves in order to receive an unbiased reading. The more upset and emotionally distraught you are when giving a read, the more off and unclear the reading can be. Be clear minded, centered, and relaxed when giving a reading whether for yourself or another. This is another reason why readers generally do not give readings to those they know whether it is an acquaintance, friend, or family member. They may unknowingly alter the reading to positively favor their friend. This is doing an injustice because you're giving false hope.

Reading for a friend can also cause friction if the friend is not positively receptive about it or ends up criticizing the read. I've heard numerous cases and have close psychic medium friends who have watched friendships and connections end over a reading that was given. Some are uncomfortable when their friend is seeing challenging circumstances and stating it to them. I've certainly had this issue myself in the past, especially considering the way I communicate let alone read in general, which can be direct and bold.

Many professional readers, psychics, and mediums have been known to obtain readings from other professionals in their field for clarity. Although, a well-known Medium friend had once said to me, "You read better for yourself than I've seen anyone do."

I'm a believer that anyone can read better for themselves than anyone else when they are in a clear state of reception. I've gone to readers in the past and found that my own readings for myself were the ones that transpired and came to light. Because in the end who knows you better than you do! Even when I have read for myself, I'm not bending the read to suit me, but rather giving myself the cold hard truth. I have given myself readings in the past that were not pleasing, but ended up coming to fruition. This is also part of the reason I moved into the spiritual teaching work. It was to help others come to the answers on their own.

I've watched others express disdain or unhappiness when they've pulled a Tarot card that appeared negative to them. Challenging is the more appropriate word. Everyone is challenged in their life. No one is exempt from that including the rich or famous. When you're challenged, then you grow and evolve. You also learn how to attract in what you desire. If a challenge is presented to you, then find ways to move through it.

The Tarot can help as a guide in terms of offering suggestions of what's to come, but in the end every human soul has free will choice. If you make a choice that goes against what the Tarot presented, then you alter the read and wind up creating a new path to head down. This is beneficial if you are faced with challenging cards, which you objectively look at as areas where you need to make some changes. The Tarot can also give you a warning, which helps to pre-armor you with what's to come. I've certainly seen the end of a personal love relationship with the Tarot weeks before it took place.

The Tarot is not necessarily going to tell you what you need to do. It is up to you to decide that for yourself. When reading for others you want to avoid telling someone what to do. You don't want to interfere with another's free will. The ethics of an exceptional reader is to present what you're picking up on without judgement, but you cannot and should not make the ultimate decision for someone else. You simply say, "If you stay with this person, then this is what I see, but it's up to you on what you ultimately decide to do."

How to Conduct a Reading

Before conducting a reading, ensure you are in a centered, calm, and focused state of contentment. This will bring you the most accurate reading. If you're not in that state, then wait until you are. The way others read varies from one person to the next. Work on finding exercises to partake in that will assist in bringing you to that calm state.

One way can be to set up a personal altar or space you use for readings. If you don't have any space in your home, then designate one in a place that is uncluttered. This is where you are most comfortable and will be undisturbed during the course of the reading. Whether that be on your bed, living room couch, or dining room table. Make sure there are no distractions when you choose to conduct a reading. You can turn this space into your own private temporary altar. You may choose to Sage the space before a reading to clear away all the negative energies. Create a calming sanctuary with candles burning, soft music playing, and incense burning. Lower the lighting a bit if you're able to.

Meditate for a few minutes or more before a reading until you are in a centered relaxed state. Take long deep breaths in and out as you relax, then say a prayer or personal invocation. Call in your Spirit team, God, your angels, guides, or whoever it is that you have a strong relationship with on the other side. When in doubt, call in your Spirit team to assist you with the card reading you're about to do.

While it's not always necessary to create all of these bells, whistles, and theatrics, you will find your readings are clearer when you create the perfect environment within and without before conducting a reading. When you pose a question to the Tarot, and find the response to be unclear, then re-word the question. If your questions are scattered, then the messages will be too.

Spreads

My soul is the core instrument I use to communicate with Heaven. It is a clear enough conduit that it's all I need before anything else. When I used to offer professional readings I'd hold the deck in my hand answering the person's questions without consulting the cards. I need to be doing something with my hands, so this is when I'd start shuffling the deck, "Let's double check everything I've said." One by one the cards would confirm it all.

I adopted my own methods from an early age by using a personal rhythm that is nothing like the default set way that others have been trained to do when reading. I've never followed the norm or anyone else's formula, but rather throw cards down like a poker player in a fury. The instant message pops up a second after the card has hit the table.

I have also never used or worked with a Tarot spread in my life. I come to the information, messages, and guidance that is intended to come through without any obstacles and restrictions. I'm a Wise One who doesn't follow anyone else's set pattern or rules. Those that know me best know this to be true. This doesn't mean that this is the way to go. This is merely what works for me. If you are in the beginning stages of reading, then you may want to investigate if spreads are something you would be more comfortable using. This is a book that is geared solely on the basic potential meanings of a Tarot card in a reading, rather than every aspect of the Tarot and how to conduct readings.

Those who have been super close to me for eons have all pointed out over the decades that they can tell when it's me communicating with them, or when it's one from the higher realms coming through. They've pointed out a distinctly noticeable shift in the language and information that comes out of me that changes within a matter of seconds. It's as if they're having a conversation with six people!

As I'm posing the question to my Spirit team, I will hear through Clairaudience how many cards I'm being asked or guided to pull for the answer and I stick with that. Trust how many cards you are guided to pull when you ask your question before you conduct a reading. Changing that number because you're unhappy with the cards that were revealed smears the reading. It ends up inaccurate and confusing. If you're unsure how many cards to pull, then stick with anywhere from 1-3 cards per question.

Tarot card readers interpret and read the cards in differing ways. Not all readers read cards in the same way. There is no right or wrong way, but however you're guided to read the cards. Some use spreads such as past, present, future spreads, or the Celtic Cross spread. While others use no spread, but pull the amount of cards they're guided or asked to pull. A Tarot spread tells a story where each card emphasizes or gives new meaning to the cards that follow or surround it.

For example, in a love read you have the Two of Cups card showing a romantic relationship, but to the right of that card is the Tower card. This might show that the relationship may be significantly altered in a way that is not necessarily welcomed, but in the end will benefit all involved even if that's not seen right away. Whereas if the card to the right of the Two of Cups is the Four of Wands, then this can indicate that the love relationship is predicted to grow stable, committed, or secure. This means that marriage can be introduced or a stronger commitment between two people.

Once you have the number of cards you're intended to pull in your mind, then shuffle the cards, and place each one face down. If you're guided to pull four cards, then that will be all you pull. Avoid continuing to pull cards after you've pulled the four cards. The only reason you would pull an additional card beyond what you were guided to pull is to obtain additional clarification on the spread already given. At that point, you would not pull more than one or two cards max. The reason is this also smears the read and causes confusion. If you're still receiving uncertainty in the reading, then start over by asking the question a different way and re-shuffling.

If you receive the same cards repeatedly over the course of time for yourself or someone else, then this is a card to pay attention to. It is emphasized and repeatedly put in front of you for a reason.

In a reading spread, the cards may either show something that already took place, is happening in your life now, or is coming up. It's up to you to determine where it falls in the time frame. If it's in the future, or has not happened yet, then this is the probable future. It is foreseen that this is what is to come. Your future changes based on the decisions or indecisions you or others make based on free will. Therefore, it's equally important not to take a future forecast read too seriously.

Many professional readers tend to state that all reads should be taken with a grain of salt or used for entertainment purposes. They cannot be held liable or responsible for a read that did not come to fruition, or for influencing the person they're reading for to make a decision that ultimately causes heartache or additional challenges. This is another reason you avoid telling others what to do in a read. Not only does it interfere with their free will choice or life path, but it can also prompt the client to make a decision that makes things worse for them. You cannot put yourself in a position where you are held liable.

The cards show the trajectory of where a situation is headed. They can also offer guidance as to what changes you would need to make in order to bring something to fruition or to prevent a challenging circumstance from happening. You own your life and the direction you choose to allow it to go in. Be the master of your own ship.

The Tarot can intimidate some who feel they'll never be able to read. It is true that some people are better at it than others the same way that some people are better drivers. Even a beginner can dominate by hitting an accurate reading out of the gate. Don't worry so much about trying to be an efficient reader. The more you let go of the need to try to be, the easier it will get.

There is nothing wrong with looking up the card meanings as you're learning, but you also don't want to base what a book says about a card as being verbatim. That goes for this book too! You most definitely don't want to conduct a professional reading for someone and then reach for a thesaurus in the middle of the reading.

Trying to learn the meanings of each card can be overwhelming. The best way to read is to not stress out over trying to learn the descriptions of each card. Instead tune into your Spirit team's guidance and follow your gut as to the first hunch you get when you flip over a card when seeing it, rather than worrying about what a card means. You may read some general meanings in this book about a card, and yet you don't see your answer that best matches your read. This is where your intuition comes in. Grasp what the overall energy and essence is about a card to help you get to the answer.

Reversals

I have nothing against reversals, while many Tarot connoisseurs rightly swear by them. You may even find along your Tarot journey that you prefer to adopt the reversals into your readings. It's a personal choice that I've chosen not to.

I don't use reversals for a couple of reasons. One of them is that I'm Clairaudient and Claircognizant, as well as Clairsentient and Clairvoyant to a good degree. I don't need the reversals as I know, hear, see, and feel what the messages are that come in when I receive a card. I'll know what the message is intended to be regardless if the card is upright or reversed.

If 1-3 cards max fall out of your deck as you're shuffling, then incorporate that into your reading. If any more than that fall out, then you're just dropping cards and none of them should be included.

If you flip over a card, or it falls out reversed, then note that this card has extra important emphasis. The impact of the message is strong with this one. If you choose to include it as a reversed card, then flip the meaning of the Upright card. For example, if it's a Five of Pentacles, which can typically indicate a challenge or loss, then reversed could show that one is moving out of the loss and things are brightening up.

There are readers who read the cards both upright and reversed, while others only read the cards upright. Both are equally beneficial and helpful in a read, but it is up to you to decide what works best for you.

If a card falls out reversed or happens to be turned upside down, I will turn it right side up and set it aside above the layout of the other cards. I know that the message in that card is exceptionally stronger than it would normally be. In the traditional Tarot, a reversed card is often the opposite of the meaning of the upright card, but not always.

Timing

Most everyone wants to know the timing of something in a reading. From Spirits perspective timing is non-existent. It was humankind that came up with clocks, calendars, and time. When Spirit attempts to relay a time frame that an Earthly being can understand, then this isn't set in stone. All souls have free will choice to act or not act how they choose.

Regardless if you make a choice or you don't make a choice, you are shifting the estimated projected time frame for an event to happen. You can also alter it completely by preventing it from happening due to free will choice. If you deny a soul mate connection and go with an entirely different soul mate choice, then you alter everyone's path including your own. This doesn't make the choice right or wrong. To an extent you are indeed creating your own destiny, even though there are key circumstances that are to take place during your Earthly life that your soul previously contracted. This also means you can push an event out into the distance from when it was originally intended to take place.

A psychic reader can state that an event will happen for someone within six months, but then those six months come and go and nothing comes to fruition. On some occasions what was projected as a probable estimation ends up coming to light two years after it was predicted.

When I was sixteen I psychically knew I would be writing books and getting into the film business at some point in my life. What I did not know for sure was 'when'. I knew the film business would come first and the writing book work would happen at some point in my thirties.   There were no doubts as I was receiving crystal clear messages and guidance from my Spirit team that would later come to fruition.

I ended up getting into the film business weeks after my twenty-third birthday. When I was twenty-eight years old, I began the process of transitioning into my book writing career. When I was in my early twenties I psychically knew I would be partaking in spiritual writing work. This was in the back of my mind, but I did not see that happening until far out into the distance. The spiritual book work was kicked off when I was thirty-seven years old. The mid-to-late thirties is when you hit your Pluto Square Pluto transit. This is the period when you experience a life changing metamorphoses and transformation. You grow wiser and view circumstances around you in a deeper way. Those that evolve and expand their consciousness at a greater rate will notice this change.

You will note by this illustration how timing was a little off for me with the work related endeavors, but the predictions did take place eventually.

I go into more detail on Psychic Timing and Psychic Insights in a couple of chapters in my book, *Spirit Guides and Angels* or in the bigger book, *Darkness of Ego*.

Tarot Card Meanings

This book can be used like an encyclopedia reference guide of the general meaning of a Tarot card, but it should not be taken verbatim. Think of this more as a gigantic cheat sheet to help direct you towards the general essence of a meaning of a card in a reading. It is up to you to add the additional layers to a reading while trusting your instincts and Spirit team's guidance and messages. They may be showing you a card because there is something on the image they want you to see. Is the human figure in the card holding a book or playing ball in a field? What could your team be telling you?

Like all of the cards in the Tarot, these are general meanings that can be applied to anything whether it be spiritual, love, general, or work. Follow your inner psychic guide on what the message is.

While testing out the cards with novices, I would throw a card down for them to tell me what they get. They would grasp the overall message coming through, but would come to this conclusion in different ways from one another. Some would point out what they were feeling when they saw the image, while others would state what they were hearing. There were those who would immediately hone in on the symbolism in the imagery such as a butterfly standing out to them. What is the symbolism of the butterfly? This helped them come to the conclusion on what the wide-ranging message was.

The meanings of each Tarot card included in this gloss over some of the basic potential meanings in a psychic tarot reading. They are not the most comprehensive or in-depth since the book would've ended up to be thousands of pages long. Nor do the definitions listed in this book mean that this is the right answer to the card and the only way it is. This is merely one reader's opinion and interpretation and meant to be used as a guide and refresher for you. You will form your own meanings of the cards outside of that by tuning into the card and paying attention to your Spirit team's communication.

Reading all of the various definitions of a card from every available source can cause confusion. Avoid getting too bogged down in the detail of the various different meanings of a card. Focus on your own inner guide as to what comes up when you see a card. What is your Spirit team trying to tell you when you throw down a card? What is the first impression you immediately get? Stick with that and avoid overthinking it. Research decks that have images in them which you will resonate strongly with as this can assist you with your readings.

I offer the various potential meanings of a card, but I do not get too involved in the symbolism or every shred of what someone is doing on a card. It may be mentioned loosely, but the point with this book is to get to the point as quickly as possible rather than getting bogged down in a thorough examination. Tarot users utilize many varying Tarot decks that the images do not all match up. I've focused on the more traditional images from the beginning days of the Tarot in this book.

In the end, when reading the cards don't worry about not being able to remember every possible meaning of a card as it may end up frustrating you. The Tarot is a complex divination tool and no two readers read the same way. As you grow more comfortable in reading the Tarot, you'll find your own system and ways of reading that are most comfortable and work best for you.

Many novices struggle with reading the Tarot as they want to know what a card can mean in their readings. They become stuck when staring at three cards side by side. While the Tarot Card Meanings in this may be of assistance by pointing you in the right direction or general area of where to look, what is important is that you pay attention to your intuition and higher self in the end. Be a crystal clear conduit of psychic reception when conducting a reading. The more you practice and read, then the better you become.

I have many spiritually based books available that surround fine tuning your body, mind, and soul to be a stronger conduit with the other side. Some of these books are available in the Warrior of Light pocket series of books called, *Spirit Guides and Angels*, *Soul Mates and Twin Flames*, *Raising Your Vibration*, *Divine Messages for Humanity*, *Connecting with the Archangels*, and *The Seven Deadly Sins*.

An Example Reading Given to a Client

The way I read is by combining all of my clair channels as illustrated in this brief example.

A client informed me that she wanted to look at love relationships. She said she was dating two guys simultaneously and wanted to know which one is the guy. Without using the deck, I repeated what I heard my Spirit team said through Clairaudience, "Neither." I added, "It looks like one of the guys is older than you and the other one is younger." She confirmed this to be true that she is in her thirties and one of the guys was in his twenties, while the other was in his forties.

I informed her that there was another guy that was going to enter the picture, but that I didn't see him becoming anything until about a year from the point of the reading. This information came to me through Clairvoyance when I saw the visual of the following year being circled on the calendar. I picked up on the energy of another guy through Clairsentience.

The next move I made was by double checking this information or any other messages that needed to come through with the Tarot deck. While I shuffled, my Spirit team audibly requested that I pull two cards. I threw down *the Empress* and *the Hierophant*. I said, "Yes, he is the guy. I received a double yes." I went further and added, "There will be marriage (Hierophant) and a pregnancy (Empress) with this guy."

A year later, I had forgot all about the read, but the woman came back to tell me I had read for her. She didn't believe the read at the time, but changed her tune when she found everything I stated was taking place exactly a year from the reading. She informed me that the two guys she was originally dating were both no longer in the picture, and that a new guy popped up with who she had a deeper connection with. She added that they have plans to get married and have a child.

Major Arcana and Minor Arcana

✠

*T*raditional Tarot decks contain 78 cards split into two groups. One group is called the Major Arcana and the other is called the Minor Arcana. "Arcana" means secrets or what is hidden and unseen.

The Major Arcana part of the deck is made up of 22 cards, while the Minor Arcana is made up of 56 cards. The Major Arcana indicates *major* life changes and shifts taking place or being suggested, while the Minor Arcana focuses on *minor* day-to-day changes and shifts. Both the Major and Minor Arcana cards are equally important in the story that a card reading is telling.

If a reading shows mostly Major Arcana cards, then this can reveal long term changes that can take many months, or even years for the change to come to fruition. If the spread is heavy up on Minor Arcana cards, then this can show smaller day-to-day changes.

The Major Arcana cards reveal situations that will take some time to come to reach maturity. It's slower moving and discloses more long term modifications, larger significant changes, or transformations taking place.

The Minor Arcana cards showcase the immediate day-to-day wisdom and guidance surrounding situations in your life.

When conducting a Tarot reading, if you notice there are more Major Arcana cards in the spread than Minor Arcana, then this can imply that you are in the process of moving through some larger profound changes in your life that take time to move through.

If the spread has no Major Arcana cards in it, then the reading is not revealing significant large transformations or changes going on at the time of the reading. Instead, you're experiencing minor day-to-day issues that change and shift from one week to the next.

If there is an equal mix of Major and Minor Arcana cards in the spread, then this can imply both day-to-day shifts and changes contributing to longer term fluctuations.

If you read for yourself regularly, or you obtain psychic or angel reads from others fairly often, then the cards that show up become less impactful in its meaning. This is especially the case if you continue to ask the same question repeatedly. Therefore, any Major Arcana cards that show up in your spread have less of an effect than if you were to have a reading once in a blue moon.

Some measure of time needs to pass in order to assess if the reading has come to fruition. When you're reading often and asking the same question, then it's more than likely that the cards will keep changing, which only causes confusion. However, the one advantage to reading often is if you notice the synchronicity of receiving the same message to a question, then this is further confirmation to pay attention to what is being relayed.

If you're giving or receiving a read on the same question regularly, then the Major Arcana cards that show up in grand abundance can have less of an impact. This means if you're constantly asking the same question to the Tarot almost daily, then any Major Arcana cards that come up are not as potent, and will therefore signify minor shifts, rather than stronger transitions that take time to occur.

Asking the Tarot the same question daily can have a negative effect on your reading. Wait about a month before having a follow up reading on the same question. This is because time needs to pass in order to allow the reading to come to fruition. I understand how tempting it can be to keep asking the Tarot the same question daily, but this has left many frustrated and more baffled. If that's the case, then revert back to the original first reading you did on the question. Write that down in a journal or email it to yourself, then revert back to it a month later to see if the reading has transpired, or if parts of the energy have begun moving in that direction. If months pass and nothing of the sort came to pass, then re-examine the reading to see if you perhaps misinterpreted it. Look at the cards you pulled in relation to your question and see if there is another way you could have interpreted it. Otherwise, free will choice has altered your path, or the reading was not accurate.

Avoid beating yourself up if a reading is inaccurate. It will happen on occasion. This can be due to misinterpreting the reading or not being in a clear state of reception when the reading was done. Human beings have the capacity for strong psychic capabilities, but even when your gifts are at its strongest, you are not God or an all-knowing omnipresent. You will make mistakes or misunderstand a message coming through.

The Fool's Journey

The Major Arcana cards have numbers on them listed from 0-21. Some call this the "Fool's Journey". The journey begins with *The Fool* card numbered 0. This represents you moving through life as you travel through each card experiencing challenges and blessings until you reach *The World* card numbered 21.

Although the names of a Tarot card vary from deck to deck, the basic traditional names of the Major Arcana are as follows:

0 The Fool	8 Strength	16 The Tower
1 The Magician	9 The Hermit	17 The Star
2 The High Priestess	10 The Wheel	18 The Moon
3 The Empress	11 Justice	19 The Sun
4 The Emperor	12 The Hanged Man	20 Judgement
5 The Hierophant	13 Death	21 The World
6 The Lovers	14 Temperance	
7 The Chariot	15 The Devil	

The Minor Arcana

The Minor Arcana is broken out into four suits or elements similar to the elements in Astrology: Fire, Air, Earth, and Water. When the person born under the sign of that element is pushed to anger, then the way they express it is much like that element. For example: Fire turns into a heated blaze burning everything in its wake. Air speeds up into uncontrollable winds blowing in a fury knocking things down. Earth dries up, cracks, and hardens unable to be invaded. Water turns into an ocean storm tsunami destroying, eroding, and drowning all it hits. Water puts out Fire, it takes over Air, and it penetrates the Earth. Earth is the least bothered by Water in a fury, when in fact it feels liberated and alive. The Earth needs the Water to grow plants, and flowers, and thrive. Water needs Earth to have something to welcomingly catch and absorb it.

Although the names of the Minor Arcana also vary from deck to deck, the most common names are: Wands, Swords, Pentacles and Cups. The following are the elements the suits represent:

Wands = Fire *(action, energy, creativity, vitality)*
Swords = Air *(mental process, communication, thoughts, knowing)*
Pentacles = Earth *(work, money, security, home, material, physical)*
Cups = Water *(emotions, relationships, social, friendships, moods, love)*

Each suit in the Minor Arcana is numbered 1-10 with four Court Cards.

The Court Cards

There are four court cards in each element suit. The traditional names are Page, Knight, Queen, and King. They can represent a person or a situation in a reading. It is up to you to decipher which one it is when conducting a reading. Look to the general personalities of each card to determine how it applies to a specific person. This is regardless if the person is male or female. A male can be a Queen card if his personality traits match the Queen, and a woman can be a

King card for the same reason.

Pay attention to any Court cards that happen to be mixed in the reading as those could indicate key people who are or will play a part in the changes taking place in a circumstance. One of the Court cards could be signifying that it is you who is the considerable part of the reading.

The Court cards can also help point to potential love partners in the vicinity for those who are single. Although, I've given readings to those already in a love relationship and discovered they or their partner was engaging in deceit with another person. This includes cheating behavior or that they are questionably close to someone in the vicinity. This can mean talking or chatting inappropriately, or in ways that would cause a partner to be suspicious. Those readings later proved to be true.

When you receive a court card in a reading and it's not representing a person, then it can be telling you to take on the traits associated with that court card

The Pages can be a messenger card or it can represent a person or situation depending on the question asked. Pages tend to be a young person under 25, therefore they may lack in maturity. Pages rank the lowest in the Court, but they are important so you want to be nice to them. They might be the assistant to a big wig Superior regardless of their age, so you need to get their attention to get close to the Superior. The Pages can also have similar meanings to the Aces of that element. If you receive both an Ace and Page of the same or different element in a reading, then pay attention to that message.

Whenever you ask the cards if you're going to hear from someone, you hope you will get one of the Pages for a response as that's a yes. Each Page varies as to what kind of communication you'll get. A Page of Wands can be a passionate message, a Page of Cups can be a love related message, a Page of Pentacles can be a slow incoming message, while a Page of Swords can be a communication message via text, email, phone, social media, etc. Pages also signify new beginnings surrounding that element.

The Knights imply movement and changes happening in one's life. Just like the image of the Knight, they are always moving. In many Tarot decks, they are seen sitting on a horse with the energy of that particular Knight reflecting each element. A Knight of Wands will move quicker than a Knight of Pentacles. A Knight of Wands moves impulsively and impatiently towards something, a Knight of Swords is quick in its thinking and communication, a Knight of Cups moves quickly through emotions and feelings or is driven by them, while a Knight of Pentacles takes its time moving while focusing on building and practicalities.

The Queens are aligned with the Kings, except the Queens are the feminine nature energy that is exuded. This means a Queen can represent a man if his overall nature tends to show feminine qualities. This does not make him any less of a man. A man can be a creative artist or exceptionally psychic, which would point to him having feminine traits. The Queens are yin energy while being receptive and internally focused. They have the power to move mountains by following their inner guidance. They have varying ways of making things happen. Think of the image of a Mother who is maternal, but in different ways. Some Mothers nurture and show compassion, while other Mothers are task master disciplinarians with a schedule.

The Kings in the Tarot are the highest ranking court cards next to the Queens. When doing a love or business reading, if you get a King and a Queen card next to one another, then this is a super strong duo, power couple, teammate, etc. Remember that a King and Queen card can still be either male or female for each. Meaning the guy can be the Queen card while the woman falls into the King traits. It doesn't make them any less of a man or a woman. These are simply the dominate energy traits they tend to convey. The same goes for a love reading for two people of the same sex. You can receive two court cards in the reading that point to the both of them. If it's a King and a Queen, then you've got a power couple on your hands. The Kings have yang energy and are action oriented. They are much like an image of a Father. Like the Mother Queens, the Father Kings are paternal in varying ways. Some Fathers are stern rationalizing dads, while others are emotionally stable listening ear kind of dads with the great advice.

THE CARDS

THE
MAJOR ARCANA

The Fool

THE FOOL .

*T*he Fool card in a reading can indicate a new beginning, whether it is a new relationship, new career, or new life and outlook entirely. It's someone attracted to new experiences and adventures. The Fool loves the newness of circumstances and people. He is a bit of a gypsy, always in motion, on the go, and moving. This can be someone who tends to move residences often as they grow restless when a situation becomes too stale. They crave variety, stimulation, and new experiences.

At times, the Fool is somewhat aimless floundering from one person, place, or thing to another without any real plan. Sometimes it works out for him and other times it doesn't. He doesn't care as it's about enjoying the journey rather than the destination. One can learn from his carefree innocence and not takes things so seriously.

The Fool makes rash decisions on an impulse only to come back months later uttering the words, "I think I made a mistake." Yet, he bounces back up again and is off in search of new adventures. He doesn't allow the failure to hold him back or drag him down.

This message can also be that you are about to embark on a new journey or a new beginning in some phase in your life. It can be a new job, new home, new relationship, or new path such as a spiritual one. If you're wondering whether to pursue a new circumstance, then this is telling you to go for it. The Fool is about taking that risk without worry. It's always a 50/50 shot on how that risk might go.

The flipside is that the Fool can also be warning you to pay attention to the decisions you're making as you could make an error in judgement. This is seen in the traditional Fool image where he is about to walk off the cliff as he frolics along carefree amused looking upwards instead of ahead. Surrounding cards would tell you more of the outcome.

For instance, if you're asking about a new job endeavor and you pull the Fool with the Eight of Cups. This could show the job experience resulting in you leaving disappointed. Another way to interpret that would be you're leaving a disappointing situation and walking into a better one. If it's the Ten of Cups with the Fool, then this shows that the experience will be emotionally fulfilling on all levels and will work out as intended.

The Fool makes spontaneous decisions without concern of the consequences. This has its repercussions at times, but the point to him is all about enjoying the journey knowing that it might not work out. The Fool is a big optimistic dreamer and usually isn't concerning himself much over what could go wrong. The flipside is that the endeavor turns out to be a success. The meaning of the Fool is to just do it. There is no mountain he cannot climb. He always feels as if he's on top of the world!

If this reading is about a new love, then the Fool can show that there is a new love relationship coming in if it's not already here. If the card is to represent another person or you, then this is someone who is possibly naïve, innocent, a free spirit, adventurous, but this person can also be uncommitted or inexperienced. The connection may not last as long as you hope when the Fool suddenly gets the urge to move on to something or someone else.

The Fool is happy, carefree, go lucky, always on the go, much like a gypsy who flits from place to place and experience to experience. He's not necessarily committed or ready for a relationship, but the cards surrounding the Fool can show if it moves into something serious. This person can indeed be very committed for life, but they have a free spirit outlook to things. They might take off for a couple days to go hiking on an island without mentioning it. He likes to be by himself quite a bit. Living in his head painting pretty pictures of dreams he wants to come true are at the top of his list. This is a whimsical, yet positive character who takes his time to stop to smell the roses. This also means he shows up late to appointments since he is easily distracted.

This is someone who others might accuse of having his head in the clouds or that he's directionless. They might say, "Put down the beer, so you can think more clearly." The Fool is always dreaming up ideas, but doesn't always act on them. He may start something new only to discover he has another idea or doesn't want to do it anymore. The Fool is the starting of an idea or endeavor, but it needs to be developed.

Sometimes the Fool can be committed pending he is with someone who can deal with his on the go independent nature. The Fool wants to feel free. He'll return home if he knows he is with someone who won't be nagging him whenever he takes off to experience the world. He needs to be with someone who is patient, understanding, and allows him space and the freedom to explore. This is not to be confused with infidelity. Texting him non-stop on his whereabouts will only drive both you and him mad. Someone will leave and it's generally the Fool who makes that move in the end. The Fool will stay as long as the reigns are not tight.

The Fool might be someone who is not yet ready to settle down. If he does commit to you, he may always be on the go. He has his own activities and interests that he often prefers to do alone. The Fool can also reveal someone who is dating around or wanting to be independent and free. This does not necessarily mean cheating. Some people like to go out and live their life, and then they come back to the home base. They are still fully committed even when they're gone for weeks at a time.

If you're currently single, then this can indicate that a new love relationship is coming to you, but remain optimistic, carefree and detached about it.

The Fool has the world at his feet and it's ripe for the picking. He is free to head in any direction he desires and isn't concerned much about the costs. The consequences are of course to look before you leap. If you are on the serious rigid side, then this is a message to lighten up and enjoy life.

If you're currently in a relationship, then this can show that the connection may take on a new positive phase. It would be a new beginning in the relationship that feels freeing for the both of you. If you are having some discord or issues within the relationship, then this card can be about one or the both of you lightening up and inviting more spontaneity into your connection.

He's not really a fool, but some might think so when they see him going after something that may or may not result in him falling flat on his face.

The Fool can point to innocence, naivety, taking a leap of faith, new beginnings, having a happy go lucky nature, taking risks without worry, becoming independent, someone who is uncommitted to anything or anyone, being spontaneous, or being playful and awakening your inner child.

The Magician

The Magician is a mover and a shaker. He is a strong communicator with the gift of knowing. He has the ability to manifest and make things happen depending on where he directs his will. This means if his mind is plagued with negative thoughts, then this is going to bring more of that to him. While this is the case with everyone in general when it comes to manifesting, with the Magician it's even more powerful. This asks you to be careful with your thoughts, feelings, and desires. Because what you put out there now will come back to you tenfold. It's always best to work on shifting your thoughts towards something positive.

The Magician says you have what it takes to obtain what you desire. You are a powerful manifester with the tools to bring what you desire to fruition. Trust your thoughts as Divine communication may be coming in through your Claircognizance channel. This means that the Magician is a positive sign that what you desire is manifesting. If you're asking about a career move, then this is a positive message that if you want what you're asking about bad enough, you're going to get it. You have power, creativity, focus, and strength of will.

The Magician follows the *Fool* in the Tarot. With the Fool, you were embarking on a brand new life without any plans and with the world at your feet. Yet, with the Magician you have a plan and it is time to put that into action. The Magician says to take your ideas and get to work on making them happen. If it's a relationship you want, then go for it. If it's a job you have your eye on, then go after it. If it's an increase in finances you desire, then think outside the box and look at other ways to make extra income. It will come naturally for you once you dive on in. The Magician isn't about sitting around waiting for something to happen. It's saying that you have all of the tools necessary to help you accomplish or obtain what you desire.

The Magician is a powerful manifester and an incredible manipulator. He is extremely gifted, creative, and strong willed. He can bring anything he wants into his life by the sheer power of his mind and easy attracting in abilities.

On the negative side, the Magician reveals a skilled con-artist and schemer. He can pull the rug from underneath you before you've noticed that you were taken advantage of. If the Magician shows up with challenging cards, it can be a warning that now you see him and now you don't. The Magician is also that smooth fast talking salesman that can make everything sound great.

The Magician is tremendously exceptional on so many levels. Depending on where he directs his attention or services, he will without a doubt of fear conquer and achieve it. This is regardless if the nature of what he desires is good or bad. The Magician operates from the deep caverns of his creative mind and understands the power of how like attracts like.

You can manifest and have what you want, but you have to put in some effort. This is about the power you carry within to make your dreams come true.

In love, the Magician card can show a magical committed union with the object of your desires. If you're having love troubles with someone, then this card is saying that you both have the willpower to make some positive changes that will benefit the both of you. This card is all about effort so action is necessary.

This can also be a warning that there may be deception at play or someone has an ulterior motive. This includes cheating or some kind of betrayal in the mix if it's next to the Three of Cups or Seven of Swords. If you're asking if a lover is faithful and you receive the

Magician card, then this might show that the person you're with could be a bit of a player. This is especially the case if it's next to the Seven of Swords card, then this is a double whammy implying that your lover is not committed in the relationship. Sometimes it's not necessarily that they're cheating, but that they don't completely feel as if they're in a relationship with you. They're not fully committed in mind and heart. They might secretly have one foot out the door and may make excuses to keep you close while not committing completely.

If you're asking about a particular person of interest you're not involved with, but you would like to find out what they're like, then this card can reveal someone with immense magnetism and charisma that naturally draws in admirers. This person has an outgoing agent or manager personality. He is extroverted and forthright dominating everyone in the room with his fast talking wit.

The Magician has a beautiful way with succeeding and winning over people and circumstances. This is someone who understands how the law of attraction works. When the Magician wants something, he often gets it through his unbending optimism and crafty ways. This card is generally a positive message that suggests that you go after what it is you want, because you will get it.

If you ask a career related question and the Magician is next to the Chariot, Nine of Pentacles, Ten of Pentacles, or King of Pentacles then this indicates that any great ideas you have conjuring up within you are divinely guided and will bring in the monetary rewards. If it's next to the Wheel or the World card, then this is also a positive sign that circumstances are changing for the better.

The Magician is a highly intelligent person. He's creative and successful, or has the abilities to manifest those character traits. He's able to take ideas and turn them into a profit. He's magical, charming, and sexy. For the most part, the Magician is typically an optimistic card that positive changes are on its way. Gifts and blessings will be bestowed on you. He takes ideas, turns them into action, which then brings on the success.

The Magician is someone who is crafty, creative, successful, manifesting, and clever. This card can be attributed to powerful creative people. It's not uncommon to see this associated with entertainers, inventors, and politicians. Entertainers and inventors are the more positive side to this creatively powerful card, while politicians associated with this card might show a trickster in office successfully deceiving the public. Some of the more positive people that this card is aligned with are people like: Steve Jobs, Henry Ford, Bill Gates, Oprah Winfrey, Walt Disney, Madonna, Steven Spielberg, Thomas Edison, and Socrates.

The High Priestess

THE HIGH PRIESTESS

*T*he High Priestess can represent someone extremely psychic, intuitive, insightful, or deep. This is someone with strong Clairvoyance that knows the answers. They might be a combination of a Medium and a Writer, or someone who has an equal amount of left brain and right brain activity. This is a thinker with just as much feeling. It can be someone falling into the role of teacher, detective, or counselor.

Like all Tarot cards, the High Priestess can represent any gender regardless if the image is of a woman or a man. Genders in the spirit world are energy rather than anatomy. This means having masculine or feminine traits, rather than being a human man or woman. Neither are more important than the other. What is key is finding balance between exuding both masculine and feminine energies.

The High Priestess stands at the gate of the physical world and the spirit world, yet there is a detached coldness to this person. You have the ability to tune in to spirit and discover the answers to most any issue. You can effortlessly dive into the deepest depths of symbols, meanings, and truth. You're not jarred by this truth no matter how harsh the tone is.

The Full Moon often depicted with this card is a message that calls for you to awaken your inner wisdom and insights. This is about getting in touch with your emotions and letting you know that you already know the truth. The truth is the first gut, hunch, or impression you received. If it is unclear at the time of the reading, then the truth will be revealed on Divine timing.

When this card shows up in a reading, you are being asked to move within and tune into your higher self, as this is where the real answers live. This is about trusting your own instincts. Your psychic gifts are working on optimum levels and you don't need the cards to seek an answer to your question, since your higher self already knows the answer.

This can be a challenging card at times because of its vague ambiguity. There is both a dark side to the messages buried inside it. It can indicate that not all has been revealed to you yet, but it will at the right time. What might be discovered can be either positive or challenging. There is a secret or something hidden, which is the missing piece to the puzzle that will answer your question. This is also a message of having patience and that you're not meant to know the answer at this time.

In love, this continues with the theme of something hidden that you are unaware of or a truth you suspect. If you're asking about a particular person you're interested in, then this message can be that the attraction you're feeling is mutual. It can indicate someone who is a mysterious psychic intuitive, or someone that will be a teacher for your soul or you for them. You and this other person will awaken deep parts of your souls together.

You may be suspicious that your partner is not faithful to you and you receive this card. This card can either mean that your hunches are accurate, or that your insecurities are ruling you and you're incorrect. This is why this card can be complicated and confusing. Surrounding cards can add additional messages of the general direction the answer is located in.

The ultimate message of The High Priestess is about having patience and waiting for the truth to be revealed. You don't need to go out searching for the answer as it's going to come naturally and at the right time. Every soul on the planet has some degree of psychic abilities. These abilities mean that you have a communication line with a Spirit Guide and Guardian Angel around you. Tune into this frequency in order to pick up on the assistance they are giving you in terms of the message you seek in this reading.

The Empress

*T*he Empress is femininity personified representing the birth of something, such as a pregnancy, the birth of a child, a new relationship, new project, new career, and so on. It is the beginning of something great! The card's essence points to this beginning as having the potential for incredible success. It will bring a fruitful abundantly happy time.

If you're asking about a particular project or endeavor you're interested in going after, and you receive the Empress, then you can be assured that it is a big yes and to go for it. There will more than likely be positive rewards as a result. The rewards can be financial or emotional. This is also the card of children or someone who is great with young people. It can be a supportive teacher or a maternal figure, regardless if it is a man or a woman.

If you're asking about a potential love interest you have your eye on, then this card would show that this person you're asking about is a nurturing soul who will care about you intensely. This is someone you'll have a reciprocated deep loyal connection with. It will more than likely lead to marriage or a long term commitment depending on your choices.

This is a blissful unconditional relationship where both people are generous and giving to one another in some way. It'll also point to the connection being a beautiful sensual union or they have a big sexual relationship. This is the pleasure card that alludes to a couple who naturally awakens the senses in the other. It can also show someone who is an artist in a creative field such as music, film, or books. This can also reveal a sensual or physically attractive person. Someone pleasing to the senses in some way.

If you're already in a relationship, then this card can have several different meanings. It may reveal that you have a strong physically intimate connection with one another. If you feel you don't have that with your partner, then this could be advising you to awaken and open up this portal. It can urge you both to pay more attention to one another. This is what the relationship needs to continue thriving. It can also show that you may likely have a child together soon, whether through adoption, surrogacy, or other avenues.

If this is a general read for yourself and this card is pulled, then it can be urging you to take a retreat into nature, take a vacation, have some "me" time, pamper yourself, think more highly of and take care of "you" inside and out, or awaken your creative talents by diving into an artistic hobby.

The Empress indicates a healthy sexuality or sex life. This is someone who loves love and physical expressions of this love. The Empress with the Emperor card in a love relationship is a power couple. It's a successfully balanced relationship between two people where there is just enough feminine energy as there is masculine. This is regardless of the genders involved.

The Empress points to creativity, art, children, sensuality, beauty, joy, fun, pregnancy, laughter, productiveness, love, nature, pleasure, high self-esteem, marriage, excellent beginnings, generosity, compassionate, and deep connections.

The Emperor

THE EMPEROR.

*T*he Emperor in the Tarot is all four King Court cards wrapped into one. He is the King of all Kings. He's intelligent, communicative, driven, passionate, and practical. The Emperor is plopped up on his throne relaxed and content, yet his demeanor conveys someone who is a leader and in complete charge. This person is extremely smart with rock solid strength. This is someone others lean on for wisdom.

When the Emperor shows up in a read, then this might indicate an authority figure around you who can be your boss, a romantic interest, or even a helpful friend. Typically, this is an older person, but it can be someone who is 30, wise beyond their years and successful. This is a grounded, protective, and loyal individual who can be male or female. This can also represent a teacher, sage, Wise One. It may even represent you.

If this read is about you, then the message is to be assertive, confident, and to go after what you want. Allow no doubt or fear to enter your mind. The Emperor rules with logic, rather than the heart. He's a thinker and a doer. The Emperor is difficult to impress and rules with an iron fist. He's the man or woman you see running corporations as CEO's and executives. These are take charge kind of people.

In a reading you may be asked to take control of your life and use precise decision making. The Emperor message can tell you to get organized, create some structure around you, and be the leader your soul was born to be. This is someone who is fearless and doesn't shy away from taking a risk. If you want to date someone, go after them, and ask them out. If you want to start a new business, then do it! This is a big yes card to whatever you're asking about.

If you're inquiring about a potential mate and what they're like, then this card shows someone who values long term relationships and commitment. This person is successful in some manner and appears or comes off totally together on all levels. They value traditional connections that go the distance. This person is likely older and wiser. If they're younger than you, then the key traits that person will have is they are extremely intelligent, successful, and already established.

The Emperor has no fear, doubts, or hesitation. When he wants something, he goes after it. When you pull this card on you, then it can be asking you to be confident, strong, have willpower, be a leader, and commit. On the more challenging side, the Emperor can be possessive, strict, perfectionist, dominating, or allows no room for mistakes.

The Hierophant

THE HIEROPHANT

*T*he Hierophant can indicate blessings being bestowed upon you.

This is usually in the form of wisdom or knowledge. It also advises one to play by the rules or follow a traditional or conservative structure in terms of the question being asked. The Hierophant could be telling you to do more research, take a class, or join an organization in the field of your interest. This is the higher learning or spiritual growth card. It is a wise person or teacher coming into your life who will be delivering the messages you need to hear. This person is a guide holding your hand.

This can also be indicating that you will unlock the knowledge you seek on your own or through a wise party. This can show someone taking a deeper interest in spiritual or faith based pursuits. They may be into higher learning or philosophical studies.

In love, this card can indicate marriage or a stronger commitment coming up on the horizon. If it's describing a relationship between two people, then this card is commitment personified. The two people are dependent on one another. This isn't to be confused with co-dependency, but this is where the couple effortlessly gravitate towards one another regularly without any issues. They are a drama free easy going couple. It's reciprocated devotion where there is no guessing where one stands. Usually this might show a couple who both value committed long term monogamous relationships. They both may be a spiritually based couple and enjoy those pursuits together. They also might be a couple who learns from one another, such as a teacher-student type relationship, whether it's love or friendship. One is more of a "know it all" teacher and the other is like a sponge starving to absorb the teacher's energy.

The Hierophant is a great card to get for someone looking for a commitment. This shows a marriage like relationship regardless if you actually tie the knot or not. It's two people dependent on one another, but in a healthy way. They're both in it for the long haul while valuing long term connections. Even if it's a sexual relationship, it will take upon a married couple like role. This is two people who share the same views, ethics, and values. They have similar interests and goals. They're both teacher and student for one another. These two people go the distance together learning valuable knowledge while evolving in the process.

If you're single and wondering what a potential partner is like, then this card could show that this person is either wise, spiritual, traditional, conservative, and/or commitment ready. They share the same values and beliefs as you. This is a highly important trait because going after someone solely based on their looks doesn't determine longevity. The Hierophant points to a love partner who shares a good deal of your interests, values, and beliefs. It's someone who would be a best friend as well as love partner. It's the best of both worlds. This person can be into religious or spiritual based pursuits, or have some connection to that. It is a value that has great importance to them.

The Lovers

THE LOVERS.

*T*he Lovers card is balancing the light and dark as well as the masculine and feminine aspects of oneself. The message in this card can show a deep loving bond between you and someone else. It's a strong physical attraction that goes beyond lust, but rather is an all-encompassing love connection where the love exists on every level possible. If there is a perfect love, then "The Lovers" is it.

While this card is the deep love relationship card in some reads, other times this has to do with choices or a major decision needing to be made. This is a Major Arcana card so the choice would be something that will effect one's long term trajectory. Perhaps one is looking to buy a home and is debating whether or not to stay in the city they're already in. Maybe they make the choice to move to an entirely different part of the state, country, or world altogether. This choice will have a profound long term effect.

If this is a relationship reading about someone already in the picture where you feel a disconnect with, then this card can be telling you that communication is needed to bring forth a stronger bond. It can be indicating that a love partnership is a big part of the basis of who you are.

If you're single, then this card is good news that a love partner is on its way into your life. This is a happy love partner card so it will be someone you are deeply compatible with or who compliments you if it is an opposites attract set up.

If you were getting together with an ex who you still have feelings for, then this could point to the meeting being positive. You both grow closer while hanging out and spending quality time together.

You have a crush on someone who you frequently bump into wondering if there is a mutual attraction. When you pull this card, then this is confirmation that your crush is attracted to you as well. While this is a promising card that there is potential for this to lead to marriage or a long term relationship, the surrounding cards in a reading can assist in showing you where this connection is projected to go.

If the Lovers is next to the Devil card, then this might say that all is not what it appears to be. It may indicate a deep attraction that is bathed in some kind of addiction. The addiction can be with one another, which would make it co-dependent. If this card is next to the Nine of Cups or Ten of Cups, then that would further solidify that this is the long term relationship you've been waiting for. If you both get together, it has the potential to go the distance. It is a healthy, committed love union.

There is usually an angel depicted on the Lovers card overlooking the two people on Earth. This is a divinely guided, orchestrated, and an inspired connection. It is a love soul mate partnership and one that is intended to connect with you. If you're dating around and this card comes up, then you have a choice to make. There is one potential who is the right choice in the mix.

This card also indicates a passionate sexual connection, one that is connected in harmony and bliss. For the most part this is a positive card unless it falls upside down reversed, or is next to challenging cards, then this message can be the opposite of harmony. Ultimately, the Lovers can reveal a deep soul mate twin flame connection. This is a union that is balanced with an equal amount of masculine feminine energy. It can also point to a major choice needing to be made.

The Chariot

THE CHARIOT.

*T*he Chariot points to great victory and accomplishment. This message also reveals swift and rapid movement towards something. Because this is one of the fast movement cards, it can therefore indicate a vacation on the horizon, a road trip, or moving residences. It might be a message guiding you to take a trip, even if it's a weekend trip sabbatical around town. This can also indicate moving rapidly towards your desire. What you desire is coming to you fast.

The Chariot says that you need will power, determination, extreme focus, and dedication. You will reach victory only if you do something about it and apply action to assist it along. Sitting on the couch all day doing nothing won't make it happen.

If you have an interest in someone, then make a move and talk to them. If you want to open up a successful business, then go for it and take steps to making it happen. The message in this card tends to point positively in your favor pending that you take action. What you want will happen, but you will need to put in some effort. It is the card of triumph should you put in that effort.

Will the new business I started do well? This card shows that it will be a major positive accomplishment and a success. You have determination to make it happen, therefore it will. Will I obtain the love I desire? This card says yes the lover you desire is on its way and coming into your vicinity rather quickly. This new person will be determined to connect with you, or you will be determined to connect with them.

The Chariot in a love relationship read isn't exactly the most romantic, but it's also not necessarily negative. The challenges to this card are that the metaphorical image of the Chariot riding quickly forward means that there will be bumps on the road that you might not see. However, you will overcome them with perseverance.

If you're single and inquiring about some traits that an incoming love interest might have, then the Chariot shows them to be a successful person. They are always on the go, moving forward, innovative, loyal, and with a strong force of purpose. They might also be a workaholic or a successful entrepreneur. If a relationship with someone ended, then this card message is instructing you to toughen up and continue on with your life in the right spirit. You will get through it.

If you're wondering how a relationship will go, then it depends on the surrounding cards. If there is a challenging card, then this can show rapid movement towards a disappointing ending. If it's a positive card, then this can indicate rapid movement towards a desirable and fantastic reward. If it's a single card, then this is a strongly favorable outcome that you will obtain what you desire.

The typical image of the Chariot shows a man sitting upright, strong, bold, and centered as he directs a chariot forward. One of the horses is black while the other is white showing duality, opposites, moving in different directions. If your relationship is rocky or you're not sure where you two stand and this card shows up, then this can be saying that strength of will is required by both partners in order to make the connection succeed. It may indicate that you both have a determination and interest to re-ignite the flames in the connection. It might also point to you both being opposites. This duality has you both taking off in different directions. You love each other, but you're vastly different. Compromise is needed to meet somewhere in the middle to make it work. The Chariot message says that what you desire will happen with effort.

Strength

*T*he Strength card illustrates compassion, inner strength, patience, and forgiveness. It says that strength is even more powerful when you go with a softer approach. The Strength card typically has an angelic woman taming a wild beast - usually a Lion. The lion is ferocious and can represent the darkness of your ego, but in the presence of the figure, it appears gentle, controlled, and under her hypnotic influence.

If this card is pulled by a tempestuous person, then it could be advising them to come at things with a kinder and softer approach. This is what real assertive strength is. If there's something you want to go after and you receive this card, then this is saying to remove doubts and go for it. The message is also asking you to exude self-assured, compassionate, confidence in all your dealings.

In love relationship reads many have admitted to being confused by this card. It's all things connected to "Strength". What does someone think of you in relation to love and romance? If you pull the Strength card, then this can show that they have an intensely passionate draw towards you. This card reveals a sexually passionate attraction, but a healthy, magnetic, sexual attraction that also involves love. It's not just about sex, but it is love intertwined with it. This potential is super drawn in to you on all levels! They have a strong attraction to you, but they might not necessarily say it out loud. When someone has a strong attraction to someone, they don't always say it. They become shy and giddy. They're afraid to say anything unless they're certain the other person is into them too.

Are you trying to get over an ex or a past love? This message asks you to work on forgiving this other person for anything you feel they caused you, or forgive yourself if it was you who did something. In this case, you're the beast/lion in the image and it is the Divine trying to ease your heart of upset, anger, hurt, or sadness.

The Hermit

The Hermit holds a lantern to light his way through the cold snow storm. He has immense psychic intuition as he moves through significant peaks and valleys in his life that contribute to his incredible spiritual growth. When the Hermit shows up in a reading, it can be saying that you're spending too much time alone or that you're not spending enough time alone. Every now and then it is necessary to have some alone time for introspection and soul searching. When you've been through a rough and challenging time, it's best to break away and be by yourself to clear your mind and allow your Spirit team to work on you. The gifted and the ultra-sensitive have no problem being alone and in fact revel in the opportunity.

There are those who go crazy whenever they are alone as they crave constant human stimulation, attention, and interaction. Having too much human attention and interaction can distract one from delving deep into themselves for the answers that await. Too many distractions also include paying too much attention to the media. The Hermit says that it is time to disconnect and take a break. This is in order to revive your soul and awaken the answers residing within you.

The challenging aspect to the Hermit is that it can be warning you that you've been experiencing too much isolation and you need to get out there into the world again. Isolation brings on stagnancy and loneliness, which are feelings that block heavenly messages. If you've been wondering when a relationship will show up, the Hermit may be saying that you've been spending too much time alone and need to get out there and find ways to connect with others so that you have a greater chance of meeting a potential love interest.

The purpose of the Hermit is that one needs to have regular bouts of alone time to connect with spirit, which brings in guidance and soul enhancing assistance. Once that's established and gained, then it's okay to get back out there and balance it out with stimulation. This may also be indicating that it is time for self-discovery or meditation.

This can represent an old soul wise beyond their years. They have no problem being alone and will often prefer it. Socially this person tends to be introverted. They have spent lifetimes mastering their soul and increasing the never ending reserve of knowledge only to pass it on to those who are ready. Many shun the material world and head off into sabbatical's alone for personal growth. This can be another message the Hermit is advising.

For a love relationship, this can indicate that one or both partners need some alone time. Some couples spend every waking moment together, therefore separate alone time is advised on occasion to re-connect with yourself. It's like a warrior at battle who retreats to recharge and then returns stronger than before. When there are disagreements or discord in any type of relationship, then this can be advising one to stop and walk away from it. Time to be alone for awhile to cool off. It can also indicate that a partner wants to be alone or they're feeling disconnected from you.

This can also show a couple who is always alone with one another. They don't have a big social life outside of their connection. They likely prefer it that way or don't have a huge desire to expand. The Hermit in a love relationship read can point to space being needed on some level. When you detach from a situation, then insight will enter the picture.

The Wheel

WHEEL of FORTUNE.

The Wheel (a.k.a. The Wheel of Fortune) is a generally positive card that can show incoming luck, wealth, or abundance. The Wheel also indicates that one's circumstances are changing, often for the better depending on other cards surrounding it. There are cycles of life where transitions are inevitable and will be happening if they haven't already. This is about knowledge and lessons being learned or gained in the process as your life moves through these changes. This is someone moving through a major life transition or a new chapter.

The Wheel is like the planet Jupiter, which bestows luck and abundance when it is positively aspected. The message in the Wheel can show circumstances turning for the better. The Wheel is typically the only Major Arcana card in the traditional deck that does not have someone on it. This is because the answers reside at a higher level. It is Spirit working the magic and bringing what is destined to happen. This is about karma, destiny, and fate.

The Wheel spins around quickly, so it can show that the life changes will be coming in out of the blue and happening fast. On the flip side, it can also show things spinning out of control. The cards enhance one another depending on what it's paired with. The Wheel with The Lovers can show a love partner entering the picture suddenly. The Wheel paired with the Death card can show that the worst is over and the beginning of something great is coming.

If you're single, the Wheel is a positive card showing that things are changing for you and a love partner is on its way. If you're already in a love relationship and it's been rocky, then the Wheel can show things turning for the better up ahead. If your love relationship is always perfect with minimal issues, then it might show some upsets or challenges coming up, or the connection is moving through a transition.

When single and desiring a love relationship, it's important to note you cannot sit around waiting for the soul mate to ring your doorbell, you have to put in an effort too. Put yourself out there and hit potentials up, be warm, receptive, and friendly. If you have been doing that, then do it more.

If things are not going so great and you pull this card, then this can indicate that things will be getting better soon. It is also a reminder to understand that life is full of peaks and valleys. No one is exempt from that. If circumstances we're always going great, then you wouldn't learn anything. The blessings you have would be taken for granted since people tend to get comfortable when everything is blissful for years, unless they regularly show gratitude. In the end, the Wheel is usually a positive card revealing great things coming in depending on what question was asked.

Justice

*T*he Justice card in a reading points to getting what one has coming to them. Justice is being served whether good or bad depending on what you've put out there. The message can also be asking you to be fair, structured, disciplined, objective, and balanced. This card is about the truth, either speaking your truth, or that the answer you've been looking for will come to light soon.

Justice in a read can indicate anything having to do with the law, legal circumstances, the courts, or police enforcement. This means anything from business contracts being drawn up, a lawsuit, marriage, or divorce license, etc. This card can also be telling you that an immediate decision needs to be made surrounding your question.

In a love reading, if you're single and asking what kind of person is coming to you romantically, then this might show that this person works in the legal arena. They can be someone who works at a law firm, whether they are a lawyer, legal assistant, or receptionist at the company. They might be a law enforcement officer, an executive in a corporate environment, a teacher, or they work in a government or political position.

The Justice message can also be that this person is honest and truthful. They speak boldly, directly, and clearly. You're not always having to guess what they're thinking or feeling. They might be someone who is by the book, traditional, conservative. This person can be an activist fighting for the truth to be heard around an issue. This is the card of getting to the truth of the matter.

Justice can be showing what you desire in a relationship. This means you want someone who is direct and honest. Perhaps your past connections were bathed in deceit, then the Justice card would be welcoming to see that the next person will be up front with you.

If you're already in a relationship and not married, then this can show a marriage coming up, a stronger commitment, or the flipside which is divorce or separation. Because this is about justice and fairness, whatever the outcome is know that in the end it is for the greater good. This is the cause and effect card that what you do comes back to you. It can be the karmic card where what goes around comes around.

In the traditional image, the two pillars symbolize structure. The scales this official person holds indicates balance. The sword in her hand symbolizes cutting to the truth of the matter. This is a person who is a fair and balanced. For that matter, they might also be a journalist or writer who takes no sides, but is objective in their stance by listening to all parties involved. They are objective when it comes to upholding the real truth even if it goes against the majority.

The Hanged Man

THE HANGED MAN.

*T*he Hanged Man card traditionally shows an individual hanging upside down. This can be telling you to look at things from a different perspective. This can also mean that you're desiring a specific result to come about when what's to come is something different than what you're expecting. The results can either be something better than what you want, or not quite what you hoped.

This can also be saying that patience is needed, or delays and roadblocks are in the way at this time. The individual in the traditional image shows him relaxed and not in motion. There is nothing to do right now. Let go of the need to control what you want to happen. Whatever it is you're asking about needs to be waited out for various reasons beyond your control. The desires will come about on divine timing. Don't make any impulsive or reckless decisions. This urges you to reflect, take pause, and observe non-movement.

You're asking if you should move residence, quit your job, or accelerate the advances towards a new love, then the message would be to wait it out. Don't make any moves at this time. This can also be about sacrifice or surrendering. If there is conflict taking place, then let it go and surrender waving the white flag. Surrender and accept someone's viewpoint. The Hanged Man can also indicate a transition or circumstance being at a standstill.

Sometimes when you're asked not to make any moves it's because you need to be enlightened about certain situations on your own. Your Spirit team will not give you all of the answers. Inner wisdom or spiritual enlightenment needs to be gained on your own time surrounding a situation.

This card can also indicate that you're at a crossroads or turning point. The meaning here is also about coming to terms with the reality of something or someone, which is why you're asked not to make any sudden moves. The truth will soon be revealed. Let it go and pre-occupy yourself with other activities to keep your mind off the focus of your desire.

This can also show someone in isolation or homebound. If you're wondering why nothing has come about with a circumstance, but you've been residing in perpetual solitude, then this is pointing out that you do need to take action or do something to pull yourself out of your rut. You cannot wait for what you desire to fall from the sky and land in your lap by not doing anything.

In love, the message is still the same as previously stated. You might be rushing too quickly with someone new you have your eye on. The Hanged Man is asking you to take your time with it and slow down or it will backfire and disintegrate. If you're already in a love relationship, then this card can be showing that things are stagnant or stuck. Something needs to happen to shake the energy out of its current rut. If you're wondering why a partner is pulling away or revealing a lack of interest, then the Hanged Man can be that they've changed their mind on their feelings, or they are unsure of what they want at this moment. You cannot force someone to be what you want them to be or act how you want them to act. The Hanged Man is not saying there is no interest, and nor is it saying yes or no, but it can be advising you to let it go for now. When it's the right time, then movement will begin. The Hanged Man can show roadblocks or delays at the moment.

Death

*T*he Death card is one of the more feared cards in the Tarot deck, but this is misguided and misunderstood. I've watched Hollywood horror films show someone reading the psychic tarot. One of the top cards they tend to want to reveal is the Death card. They immediately write it into the storyline that someone is going to die. This couldn't be more cliché or further from the truth. They need a spiritual consultant on the sets of those movies. I've conducted readings for people in the past with them sitting in front of me. Whenever I flip over the Death card they say with horror and panic, "What-is-that!?"

The Death card is almost never about someone physically dying. The Tarot is not literal and the Death card is more positive than one might believe. Everyone is experiencing repeated deaths all throughout their lives. In all of those cases, the Death card would pop up in a read. Deaths in this equation result in endings.

In a reading, this is about endings followed by new beginnings. When it is an ending or bringing something to closure, then this opens the door to a fresh new chapter in your life. You've got a clean slate once the Death card happens.

You're clinging tightly to someone you're interested in romantically, but this person has showed no interest back. This card can be telling you to release the desire for this person because there is someone better who will be entering the picture. It may be a warning that this person you have fixation on would not be good for you in the end or they have no interest in you romantically. There is a bright new beginning coming up, but you need to let go of the old and outdated in order for this change to come about.

You've overstayed your welcome in your current residence and this card shows up in your reading. It is time to stop putting up resistance or making excuses to avoid having to move. The Death card is a powerful intense message that something that is of no use is needing to end so that something good can come in.

If you recall that moment you were going through a specific transformation internally where you traveled down a higher spiritual path, then this card would have shown up in your spread at the time. Whenever the Death card shows up, then this can indicate tons of change and transformation going on in an area of your life.

If you're single and this card shows up in a love reading, then this can be suggesting that there might be something in your life that needs to be brought to closure in order to bring this new person in. You could be hanging onto a past love or ex. It can also be a rigid mindset that needs to be released. This is followed by adopting a new positive mindset. It can also be saying that your life as a single person is over and the relationship is in the vicinity. You are at an ending of one part of your life and ready to start a new chapter where the lover enters the picture.

If you're already in a love relationship, then this doesn't necessarily mean that the relationship will be ending, although it most certainly can. The Death card will end a relationship that was unstable or unhealthy to begin with. It ends what needs to be brought to closure for your own higher good and overall well-being. If this is refused, then denial enters the equation where you make excuses that all is well, when in fact there are major unseen holes in the connection.

The flip side is that you are indeed in a happy healthy love relationship, but this card comes up in the reading. This does not automatically mean the relationship will end, but something about the union dynamic may change. There is something ending or changing within the connection. For example, you find out you are both going to have a child or will adopt a child. When there is a new soul entering a household, then that changes the current dynamic of the relationship.

This dramatic change is associated with the Death card.

You continue to despise and complain about your job, but are afraid to leave because you have bills to pay or you fear taking that leap. The Death card can be saying that you will need to do something drastic such as taking a chance and leaving this place that makes you unhappy. Do whatever you can to find another job. Otherwise the law of attraction will do it for you in ways that might not initially be welcomed, but in the end would benefit you.

I've witnessed cases where someone was laid off at their job. You give them sympathies, but they say something cheery like, "I wasn't happy working at that place for quite awhile, so this is a blessing in disguise." The Death card could have shown up in their reading spread to indicate this.

The dark imagery of the traditional Death card suggests that people are afraid of change. The skeleton is riding a horse knocking a King with a crown onto the ground. This represents stomping out the ego, which desires titles and prestige. The message suggests that you are resisting change out of fear when change needs to take place. The change is coming whether you like it or not.

Look to the surrounding cards to see where the change is evident if this is a general read. It will also indicate whether it is a positive change or challenging one.

For example, if the Death card is next to the Nine of Cups, then this could show a positive change in your love life or an ending of a connection if the Death card follows the Nine of Cups. The Death next to a Pentacles card can show a change in your finances or job. If it's next to the Page of Pentacles, then it's a smaller positive financial change. If it's next to the Ten of Pentacles, then it's a larger one. Sitting next to the Five of Pentacles can indicate a loss. Look to the way the cards fall next to one another as if it is telling a story.

The Death card is about endings, beginnings, transformations, letting go of something, releasing, change, or metamorphoses.

Temperance

The Temperance message can be telling you that the need for balance is required. It can say that you're a centered person or that circumstances are starting to balance out. The message can also point to someone who has been tempted by addictions, but is working on straightening their life out. They can be getting their toes wet in some kind of addiction or something that isn't good for them.

This can also be asking you to be the calm within the storm. Everyone around you is obsessing over drama or gossip, but you're completely composed, detached, and uninterested in any of it. The personality trait of this card is someone who is centered and balanced. The opposite is that someone can be addicted to some form of toxin intake. This card can suggest you remember to use moderation with anything that could be toxic or addictive.

You're single and interested in someone romantically, then Temperance can show that there is chemistry, but it can also be saying the feelings the person has for you are up and down. It's not stable, but changeable. This can also be the opposites attract card.

The image in the Temperance card tends to show an angel or someone pouring water from one cup to another. This indicates, balance, synastry, chemistry, flow of energy, etc. This is also the card of someone being at a crossroads or in the process of transforming their life. If a new connection doesn't seem to be forming quickly enough, this message can be saying that one or the both of you are in the middle of a personal transformation, trying to balance their life out, or bringing an addictive streak to a close.

Perhaps your current relationship has been experiencing some challenges, then the Temperance card can indicate that the connection will be smoothed out soon. The equilibrium between the couple will reach a more harmonious and peaceful state. It can also show that the connection is already a peaceful balanced one.

If a relationship is experiencing argumentative discord, then this card is suggesting that working together and compromising on the things you cannot change will bring more balance and harmony to the connection. This means having tolerance for someone. Many complaints about one's partner tend to be on the petty side. There's a great deal of trying to control what they want their partner to be. Your partner is not an object. Temperance says to relax about it and let it go to achieve balance.

The message in this card can also show a couple finding middle ground and a way to merge together despite their differences in personalities or values, etc. The negative side to an opposites attract situation is it can reveal an imbalance between two people. It depends on whether the surrounding cards are challenging or favorable.

Romantically, this can show the person you're interested in is absorbed heavily in work and that's why it feels as if you're not really connecting. If you're single, then this can be more of an internal struggle to find balance and reach a higher harmonious feeling, then the love partner will come in naturally.

In the traditional image the figure has one toe is in the water, which represents subconscious, and one foot is on land, the conscious. There is a healthy balance of both the spiritual and the practical in this person.

In a general read, the Temperance card falls next to the Eight of Pentacles. One could say that you're working too hard and that's great, but you need to find some balance so you do not experience burn out. Temperance is about moderation, balance, harmony, synergy, patience, serenity, or compromise.

The Devil

The Devil card in a reading indicates an underlying fear you may not be aware of. You have a longing desire for something or someone to the point where it plagues your thoughts every minute as if your life depended on it. The Devil can be indicating an obsession. What are you obsessing over? Obsessions border on the unhealthy side and can explode into chaos if left unchecked.

The Devil can show someone being in self-centered mode or chained down by their own desires. You are terribly fixated on obtaining someone to the point that you're not seeing that the person you're focused on might not be all that great for you. Love cannot be forced or willed to happen. Real love forms and blends gradually over time with another calmly and naturally.

The Devil can also reveal a co-dependent relationship. You are so entranced by the one you're with that it's causing or will cause you or the other person to feel trapped by it. Relationships are two people who are separate and independent, yet they come together without force or out of a need to fulfill an emotional void. When it's used to fulfill ego needs, then this is when the Devil turns up. There is an ulterior motive for you in wanting that person, even if you subconsciously feel that it is genuine. The Devil creates deception and blinders over the truth.

When you're in a co-dependent state, you are likely unaware of that. You're only feeling and thinking about what you want and no one else. The Devil can indicate an obsession over someone to the point of lust. They're likely super physically attractive or easy on the eyes. This leads one to believe that this person is the one, when in truth the Devil is warning you to not become obsessed by this person since they may not be the one. Heavily fixating on someone's exterior is blinding you to this truth. They might seem good on paper initially, but in the end the Devil is a warning.

If you're in a relationship or have your eye on someone new, then this card doesn't necessarily mean the relationship is over or will not happen, but it is asking you to evaluate your behavior and true motives or intentions with this person. Make sure it's not in the areas of toxicity. This can also indicate someone having a harmful addiction to drugs, alcohol, sex, or an unhealthy fixation on someone else. Take a step back and evaluate if it's you or the other person that this applies to. It can say that it's the both of you. This is a relationship connection governed by some kind of unhealthy obsessive addiction.

Examine the traditional image of the Devil card. It's two people nearly undressed or naked with chains around their necks. The chains are being controlled and held by a Devil figure. He stands above them with forceful power. Two human figures are cowered and submissive to him on the ground. The Devil figure is a metaphor representing your dark ego desires. You are chained and being controlled by your ego. When your ego is at the helms, then this is when mistakes are made. It can prompt someone to move through a situation with blindfolds on. Metaphorically, you have your head down not seeing things clearly. You are transfixed almost as if under a spell and therefore not seeing an issue or circumstance clearly.

You have an intense unbending crush on someone, then this could be asking you to take a step back and make sure you're seeing this person for who they are. They can be hiding something or they might not be that interested in you. When you have a deep crush on someone, then this creates a hazy fog. The repercussions can be dangerous if this person isn't that interested in you at the level that you are inside. The disappointment can be great enough to damper your day and let you down.

The flipside is this person can be sexually attracted to you, but it's on a superficial surface level. They are sexualizing you or lusting after you because of how you appear or who you are, but this isn't to be confused with deep long term love. Their interest in you is on a purely physical level. This can ultimately cause issues for the both of you. You need to have this person to the point where it hurts, or you may be desiring more than a one-night stand kind of connection with someone who is only interested in how you appear, but not who you truly are. Physical attraction does not automatically equate to long term relationship

The Devil can indicate a sexual relationship and nothing deeper. Look at the surrounding cards to see how the connection will go. For example, if you get the Devil card and the Ten of Cups next to it, then that might indicate a physical obsessive connection that later levels out and becomes a loyal loving happy relationship. If it's next to the Seven of Swords, then you've got all sorts of deception going on and it won't end positively. The Three of Swords could indicate a co-dependent connection that will end in heartbreak and disappointment. If it's next to the Three of Pentacles or Eight of Pentacles, then this might show the connection turning into a professional working relationship, or it's a hot passionate love affair that starts in the workplace. It might also indicate that this relationship is one where the both of you continuously work together to thrive and grow as a team.

The ego is an inner force within all souls representing your fears, addictions, and other harmful impulses. The ego is a master of deception and creates the illusion that you are involuntarily bound to it. The Devil can reveal that it is you who is chasing after someone and idealizing them as a potential partner, but you're not seeing this person or this possibility clearly. You refuse to stop pushing for a connection with this person until it finally ends in disappointment. This same concept applies to whatever the question is, whether it's career, family, friendships, or even material necessities.

You have the power to remove the metaphysical chains and see the real truth. This will free you from any false imprisonment you are allowing to overtake you.

Think about what you're afraid of or what addictions you have that bring you guilt. Addictions are not necessarily drugs, alcohol, or any other vice. They can be an addiction to gossip, the internet, an easy lifestyle, or anything harsh that ultimately has a harmful effect on your state of being. It is one that stalls you from continuing on your life path. It wears you down and makes you stressed, irritable, or tired. Don't let your fears take hold of you. Release negative fearful and ego based thoughts that divert you off your path or stall you from getting where you need to be. Understand that the Devil card doesn't mean something won't happen, but to be aware of the whole picture.

What does this person think of you? The Devil can show attraction in a big way to the point where they are lusting over you or deeply physically attracted to you. This person might be afraid of giving themselves over to it because it feels dangerous and insecurities can be stopping them from making a move. This doesn't mean a relationship can't happen, but a move will need to be made.

The Devil is obsessive over you, codependent, and addicted. It may show an unhealthy sexual addiction or one sided attraction with someone. It can also show someone who is ignorant or doesn't know any better. This is someone with poor judgement.

The Devil isn't love, but lust so it might delude you to thinking you're in love. The true test if someone is in love with you is if they stand by you no matter what. They've seen you at your best and worst, yet they still stay. If they end up leaving and give you the song and dance number that the feelings for you are gone, then the Devil would play well here as it was a warning that the person was super attracted to you on a lust level, but that's not love. Lust does not keep someone around.

The Tower

THE TOWER.

In the image of the traditional Tower card, it tends to depict a building being blown apart with two figures being tossed from it against their will. It's no surprise that someone might find it upsetting when they're hoping a response to a question will be a positive one. When challenges arise blessings are born. This is the case even if it's not witnessed or understood as the challenges are taking place.

The building is your perfect stable world, but it is suddenly disrupted in a major way. The crown being released and thrown in the image is symbolic of being knocked off your pedestal and losing it all. Understand that when you lose it all, it is in order to be reborn stronger and better than before.

As always with the Tarot, the symbolism in the images are metaphors. In this case, the building is your perfect solid world. It's being blown apart crumbling the foundation you've been so comfortable with for some time. In the end it's for good reason. You could be stuck in a long running rut, so the Universe decides it's going to shake things up whether you like it or not. The messages with this card are not always negative, so it's important to not jump to conclusions and assume the worst. At the same time, even if it's a warning, it's best to not live in the space of denial to what's coming, and instead prepare and armor yourself so that the transition isn't as challenging, but met with the right spirit.

If you've been feeling stagnant for a long period of time, then the Tower can be welcoming as it may bring you some major positive shifts either spiritually or physically that can break you out of the monotony.

The Tower card in a reading indicates a sudden abrupt change about to take place. You might already be in the midst of it. This change can be positive or negative depending on how you perceive it. If it's showing that a relationship or job you're in will abruptly end, then you may either be shocked by its conclusion or you might say, "I sort of suspected it."

In a love relationship, the Tower card doesn't necessarily show the ending of a connection, but it can show an ending with the current way things have been. Something jarring or abrupt could take place within one or the both of you that alters the dynamic of the connection. It can be something positive where you've been dating one another, but then something drastic happens that bonds you together on a higher level where it becomes a serious relationship. It can also show the dismantling of a connection, explosive emotional arguments, or tough times together. It might be something drastic takes place where you find that one of you receives a huge job offer in another city.

If you're single, then this card can show that perhaps the reason love has alluded you is you're in the middle of volatile inner changes that are helping you grow, then you'll be ready for this next partner.

The Tower card tends to indicate abrupt and unexpected change, which can either be a blessing or a challenge. It can show situations that have become chaotic and messy. It will reveal emotional confrontations, as well as sudden clairvoyant visions of the truth to something you've needed answers for.

This card may scare those who are typically uncomfortable with change, which most human beings are. The change that the Tower displays is radical out of the blue abrupt change, rather than a gradual process of change. You do not have to time prepare for the kind of change the Tower brings. This is why it can be jarring. It's an indication of your plans not going as you expected.

Even though this is a challenging card and can be perceived as negative, understand that abrupt change happens for a reason and that there is always a light at the end of the tunnel.

One of the positives of this card is that you've been living a life of stagnancy for six months, then this card pops up to show that something major and abrupt is going to knock that stagnancy off its axis for the better. The Tower points to major abrupt change regardless of it seeming to be a blessing or a challenge. If it shows a relationship ending, then it is a blessing in the sense that you don't want to remain with someone who is no longer into you anyway.

The Star

THE STAR.

*T*he Star card brings with it a message of hope. The stars in the sky are a symbol of reaching the light at the end of the dark tunnel. It is looking up to the Heavens and the Universe for guidance and support. It is strengthening your connection with God, your Spirit team, a higher power, or a force greater than your physical being.

The Star is an upbeat and optimistic card full of promise of good things to come. It typically shows up when a glimmer of hope is about to reveal itself that all will end well. It may show up when you've been going through some challenging times to let you know that it's smooth sailing up ahead and the worst is over. Now the healing process begins. This points to emotional or physical healing taking place. The Star message indicates a time of transcending the material and ego, and instead evolving into spiritual based pursuits. It's a reminder to not allow your faith to waver. Believe that anything is possible and that what you desire is on its way.

The image of the Star card tends to show a naked human figure with one foot on the Earth and the other foot in a pool or lake, while pouring water into it from a flask. The symbolism of water pouring into water is telling you to allow circumstances to flow freely. Things are flowing positively in your life or will be if they aren't already. The one foot planted on Earth is connected to being grounded and stable, while the one foot in the water is connected to God, a higher consciousness, spiritual bliss, or intuition. This card can also show a time of psychic insight and creativity. Trust your instincts and pay attention to the first initial hunches you receive. The nude image isn't about sexuality. The symbolism is about openness and baring your soul without fear of needing to be protected. It's about being free on all levels.

The message says whatever you've been wishing or hoping for is on its way. The Star is the green light to move full steam ahead. It indicates that whatever you desire, you can have. It's either coming on its own or will be present when you put in an effort. This is the big yes card that tells someone to go for it! It shows someone whose world is on a stage.

If you're wondering what a potential lover sees in you, then this can be indicating that they see you as a beacon of hope, an angel of light, someone who is cracked open, raw, and honest. It can also be how you see them, or that the relationship connection will be a spiritual soul connection rather than a relationship based on external desires. It is deeper than just a physical attraction.

If you are in a relationship, then expect it to brighten up. If you are looking to meet someone new, then get out there, mingle, and let your positive self shine bright. This is a cheery message that circumstances are going to improve. The Star is all about taking risks and going for it. The universe is cracked open and ready to bless you with your needs. This card is about being open to love if you're single or that a potential partner is coming to you who will awaken all parts of you. It will be an ever evolving spiritual soul mate love connection. The ultimate message says that things are looking up, so be the star that your soul was born to be. Don't allow negative thinking patterns like doubt to creep in and stall you from moving forward. Allow your soul to shine bright with confidence and be receptive to what's being handed to you. Think big and go after what you want without hesitation. Be prepared for a period of harmony, serenity, centeredness, calm, as well as powerful insights and intuitive flashes of creativity.

The Moon

THE MOON.

*T*he Moon card in a reading operates much like the Full Moon transit at times and carries with it similar meanings. It can indicate timing on a situation coming to fruition on a Full Moon or taking place at night.

When the Moon card shows up in a reading it can ask you to pay attention to your inner feelings, dreams, and emotions. It can also be telling someone that the truth or answer you're looking for will be revealed. This is about what's hidden, secrets, and the unseen. For that matter, the secrets can be dark or unwelcomed.

If you think a situation seems to be perfect, then this card may be telling you that there is something that hasn't been revealed yet that can make or break that. This is the same as if a circumstance is seemingly bad, then this card may be telling you that it's not as bad as it seems. Or that you're not seeing the whole picture and things are not as bad as you think.

The cards following the Moon give the reader an idea as to what's about to be revealed whether positive or negative.

If it's a general read and you get the Moon, and the Ten of Cups, and Lovers card, then this can indicate that there is a love relationship potential about to be revealed for you.

Without the Sun, then the Moon resides in the darkness. You need the Sun to shine a light on what is hidden. The Moon indicates secrets untold.

The Moon can also be saying that you already know the answer to the question you're asking. This is the psychic intuition card and you need to pay attention to your gut, hunches, and your Spirit team. What was the first reaction response you received on the question without second guessing it?

This card indicates anxieties, confusion, hyper emotions, depression, and fears. The guidance can be to tune into your feelings for the answers, or that clarity is needed. One's inner world might be tumultuous and the need for peace and serenity is key.

In a love reading, the Moon might show deception lurking around or heavy anxiety ridden emotions in you or another person. The card can be telling someone that they're moving through a heavy emotional time.

If you're single and have your eye on someone in particular, then this card can be showing a lack of clarity with this person. It can be that the person is not a stable partner for you. It might reveal them to be an emotional person who is in tune to the feelings of others. This is a creative person who works in the artistic worlds (photography, film, writing, etc.) The Moon may also show them to be hiding something or that there is something you don't know about them that might be a deal breaker. The surrounding cards can offer more of the direction the potential connection can head down.

If you're in a love relationship, then the Moon could reveal a deep secretive love union filled with tons of emotion. It may be saying that you or your partner is having insecurities and anxieties about the relationship. You're worrying about something negative being there that is not based in truth. On the flip side, if you think all is well, then this card can say that the person you're in love with might not be what they seem. When one is in love with someone, they tend to see that person through rose colored glasses or a hazy lens. The person is not as perfect as you're making them out to be. This is also because there is no human being that is perfect and flawless in the end. Everyone is battling with challenges, demons, or stresses from one degree to another. The Moon shows something crucial being hidden from you more along the lines of deception.

The Moon card typically shows a wolf howling up at a huge moon.

The symbolism of the wolf in the Moon card is saying you need to adapt to a situation you have no control over. Wolves are highly telepathic intelligent hunters and they follow their intuition. They are able to be alone and navigate through the darkness. This is the Moon message for you or another in a reading. Wolves are also loyal and mate for life, so this can also be a personality trait for someone in a reading. The lobster crawling out of the water is about sinking into emotional depths, but coming out of that transformed and rejuvenated. You may be moving through a rough emotional time, but it will re-ignite your soul in the process as you come out of it altered from the experience.

The Moon is about feelings, deep emotions, illusion, deception, secrets, the unseen, or feeling lost. The light side of the Moon card is inspiration, creativity, creating, coming out of the darkness, or psychic intuition.

The Sun

*T*he Sun in a reading is one of the more positive and optimistic cards to receive. It's a welcome relief that circumstances are going to be what you dreamed or hoped for. It reveals happy times on the horizon.

The previous Moon card indicated secrets untold and living in the darkness, whereas the Sun card brings everything to light. The Sun is the truth being cracked open and the reality revealed. It's being brilliant, confident, alive, joyful, and accomplished. The Sun indicates positive things heading your way.

Whether you're asking about a job you want, or about a relationship, home, or career, then this card gives the resounding thumbs up that it will be even better than you expect it to be. This is also the card of notoriety and fame where career is related. Tons of popularity is imminent on some level whether in a social circle or in general.

The Sun can also be about finding enlightenment or being informed of the truth about something. It signifies happy times are on its way and the worst is over.

In a love reading, when asking about what this incoming potential partner is like, the Sun can be saying that this person is a warm, outgoing, sunny kind of person. They walk in a room and those around are drawn to them as their personality radiates and shines brightly. This person is accomplished, playful, cheery, or successful. Everyone feels this person's love when they are focused on them.

If you're single, then this can be saying that the long term partner is coming into your life in a big way. If you're dating or in a relationship, then this card can indicate marriage or a stronger commitment. It can be a celebration or good times up ahead with this person. This can also be used as the Summer time card for timing questions.

The Sun can also be about prosperity, marriage, home, wealth, achievement, positive well-being, life force, and good health. It's the card of ultimate freedom and liberation. Even if it's showing the end of a relationship, the break will feel as if a weight has been lifted.

Where the Moon card indicated something hidden, the Sun shines the spotlight on something big being revealed. What's revealed may be what you don't want to initially hear, but because it's the Sun card, it will be followed by positive news surrounding something great. If a relationship is ending, the card can reveal that there is someone new around the corner, or that you'll be happier out of this connection than with this person, even if you don't believe that yet.

The image in the Sun card typically shows a young child happily riding a horse with sunflowers scattered around. It doesn't get any better than that. The symbolism points to a period of good times, an awakening, letting your inner child out, as well as playfulness. It's a feeling of profound freedom. Some of the symbolic meanings of the Sunflowers are longevity, adoration, joy, spiritual awakening, and good luck.

Judgement

JUDGEMENT.

*T*he Judgement in a reading indicates periods of self-reflection and transformation. This is dying only to be re-born again stronger. It can be about making sudden decisions to change your life and head off in another direction.

The typical image of the Judgement card shows a large angelic presence presiding over many graves with human beings leaping from it in rejoice. They are usually naked which symbolizes being whole and complete. In a reading, this can indicate being open, exposed, and unafraid of vulnerability. This can say that you have a reason to celebrate or rejoice about something. It can reveal a feeling of renewal.

The Judgement card usually shows up when someone is at the end of one particular journey or chapter and ready to embark on a new one. Judgement can also indicate new beginnings once you let the past go. If it's the end of a relationship, then it can be telling you to let the relationship go. It's time to move onto the next chapter.

Where the Death card can reveal an unwanted change or an ending in one's life, the Judgement card is an ending that you chose to end on your own. It is making your peace with it and looking forward to the next chapter with optimism.

Judgement can be an enthusiastic card where you have to put in tons of effort into something, and now blessings will be bestowed in return. The traditional Judgement meaning was intended to depict the Archangel Gabriel firing his trumpet which set off the day of judgement for souls crossing over. The only judging that takes place is the one that the soul places upon themselves during this time of judgement. Your perspective is much clearer when you exit the Earth plane. Your mistakes are apparent prompting your soul to wish you could do certain things over again. Judgement can be saying that there is some judging going on. Either you're judging someone too harshly or they're judging you.

I've received this card repeatedly following the breakup of a relationship. While it might indicate a break up, generally it shows up after the break up. It's a reminder that break ups happen in relationships. It's the process of human life. You cannot control why someone chooses to leave. Judgement is an indication that a relationship has ended. It is the closing of one chapter and it is time to pull yourself up and move forward fearlessly into your next chapter. This next chapter is a clean slate that can bring a new love to you. A new love can also be a renewed love with the former flame. It would be as if it is a brand new relationship even if you had previously been together before. This shows you moving through a renewal or new sense of self following a challenging situation.

If you've been having problems in a current relationship and feel a distance with your partner, then this can be showing this detachment. Your partner is at a crossroads evaluating certain things connected to the relationship. This doesn't mean the relationship is over. It can be something minor where they come back to say they were bothered by something you did or said. It can be an isolated issue that is strong enough to transform the person to some extent or make them judge the relationship. This is nothing abnormal as all couples have struggles, issues, and disagreements, unless there is one person in the duo who is agreeable to keep the peace. This card can also show a renewal or revival of a past connection. It can be a renewal in oneself, self-reflection, and transcendence.

The World

*T*he World card showing up in a reading indicates that an accomplishment has been achieved. One life cycle within a human life has been completed surrounding that area. This can be a book has been finished, you're graduating some level of school, you've just sold your house, or bought a house, you're up for an award, you've successfully completed a tour. The World is saying that everything has come full circle and successful completion has been achieved. Pat yourself on the back and celebrate. There is a sense of closure, completion, or mutual ending of something pertaining to the question asked.

The World can also be personal spiritual growth that's been achieved. This card is not always practical material success. It can be that you've moved to the next level on your journey and are ready to embark on a new one.

The Fool card is the first card in the Major Arcana that signifies the beginning of a journey, but the World card is the last card in the Major Arcana showing that journey coming to end. Rewards are indicated when anything is accomplished. Rewards are not necessarily monetary, plaques, and awards, but it's the knowledge gained that is its own reward.

The World in a love relationship reading is a positive card to get especially if it's in the future position or one of the last cards in the spread of a reading. It shows the relationship coming full circle, growing deeper, or more committed and closer. If you're single, then the World can indicate that you are coming out of that cycle and are ready for a new love. If you're asking about someone you have your eye on, then this card can be saying that this person is someone who is fully together, independent, successful, and long term relationship oriented.

The World is also the card that indicates travel, so it can be that you meet someone significant while travelling. It might suggest that you take a mini-getaway to help clear your mind of any residual toxins in order to put the chapter you're currently in to rest.

The World is equated to travelling the world, so this is where travel comes in. It can be that you're planning on taking a weekend getaway alone. If the World is next to a court card or positive love related card, then it's possible you will meet a potential lover while away if you're single.

The
Minor Arcana

Wands/Fire

*T*he Wands in the Minor Arcana represent the element of Fire. Astrologically it would pertain to the signs of Aries, Leo, Sagittarius.

Fire is action oriented, passionate, aggressive, extroverted, loud, fiery intense, creative, productive, celebratory, at war, victorious, full of accolades, struggling, strengthening, egotistical, accomplished, exciting, enthusiastic, jealous, defensive, conflicting, achieving, rewarding, delegating, popular, obsessive, or hyper emotional.

The Wand suit in the Tarot are action oriented. It's making moves or taking action steps to make things happen. What ends up happening as a result can be either blessing oriented or challenging.

The Wands/Fire element pushes circumstances forward. It puts in an effort. The challenging side to the Wands/Fire suit is when you put too much energy and enthusiasm into something that is either a lost cause or is directionless. When it's aimless, then the results end up being all over the place.

Fire can blaze uncontrollably heating up and burning everything in its wake, but it can also breathe life into something that might have been dormant or dead. When the Wands/Fire is angry, then it blows everything up creating chaos and drama. When it is positively channeled, then it is an excellent ingredient in a recipe for success and enterprise.

Ace of Wands

*T*he Ace of Wands in a reading can indicate the start of something full of energy and amazement. This can be a brilliant creative idea or the potential for an intensely passionate relationship. The image in the traditional Ace of Wands card typically shows a hand and an arm coming out of the clouds pushing a huge wand into the air. This message points to the birth of an idea that is divinely guided. The leaves and flowers attached to the wand and falling off it reveal abundance and fruitfulness coming out of this idea as a result. The Ace of Wands tells someone that an idea is a good one and you should go for it to make it happen by taking action.

While all of the Aces represent new beginnings surrounding the element of the suit, the Ace of Wands represents putting that new beginning into action. This action can bring about positive blessings or challenges depending on the surrounding cards in a reading.

Ace of Wands gives someone that fiery passionate energy moment showcasing a breakthrough. It's a light shining down on what you need to do next. When you come up with a brilliant idea, then the Ace of Wands would confirm that it is one you are intended to move forward with.

The Ace of Wands is present when there is a great idea for a business venture, a book, a project, or anything that is brought upon by the imagination or Divine guidance. If you're a writer or artist facing creative drought or a block, then this message is an exciting indicator that the resistance is over. Awesome innovative ideas are immersing out of you, so pay attention to it.

The Ace of Wands is a hyper exciting energy telling you to nab it and take action immediately. The energy rushes into your life just as quickly as it evaporates. Utilize the immediate enthusiastic energy to your advantage by doing something about it.

Ace of Wands points to an exciting and passionate new beginning. It is the birth of a splendid idea, but action is needed to make it grow and prosper. This is an exceptional card to receive surrounding creative projects or work related endeavors. The Ace of Wands points to a huge influx of positive energy much like a caffeine jolt of excitement.

Ace of Wands in a relationship love reading can indicate a strong magnetic and passionate attraction between you and the person being asked about. This is also the card of a deep sexual draw and attraction. If it's with someone from the past, then it can be a rekindling of that passion, a re-igniting of the union, or it's telling you that the attraction has never dissolved even if you had broken up or are separated. If you're single, there is an exciting passionate potential entering your vicinity.

If you're single and wanting to know the personality traits of an incoming potential, then the Ace of Wands can show someone who is enthusiastic, courageous, exciting, creative, passionate, confident, fiery, and innovative. This is someone with tons of creative ideas and drive.

Even though the Ace of Wands typically has a positive meaning where love relationships are concerned, it doesn't necessarily determine whether or not a relationship will go the distance. It's not saying that a connection will or will not happen. It is simply saying there is an interest on both ends, but one or the both of you will need to put in an effort to propel it forward. An action step is required.

In love and relationships, this points to an exciting passionate and fiery extroverted duo when in one another's presence. The Ace of Wands shows that there is a strong physical and magnetic attraction between a couple.

If you've been in a relationship that has been stale for some time, then the Ace of Wands can show a spike of excitement or some spicy passion immersing itself into the both of you. It can also be advising you to take the bull by the horns and work with your mate to re-ignite the passion in the relationship if it's been lacking.

This card doesn't necessarily show a long term connection that sustains passion. This can be an exciting date with someone on a Saturday night that fizzles out by Sunday and it's back to the grind. It is merely saying there is a mutual passionate attraction. You both have something to work with. The Ace of Wands indicates attraction and chemistry. The surrounding cards can determine whether or not it's a passionate connection that develops into a long term love relationship or if it will dissolve. This would also apply to other areas of your life.

The Ace of Wands is an excellent yes card to questions pertaining to a new career, project, or relationship. There are tons of extroverted fire expression energy with the Ace of Wands, but you need to take action on it. It's the initial birth of an award winning idea. It's the pilot light ready to be ignited with a match.

Two of Wands

*T*he Two of Wands points to someone being at a crossroads. You are facing two roads that have split off into two different directions. You have a choice to make as to which road you're going to head down. One of the roads may be more challenging than the other, but you won't know until you're on it. The Two of Wands follows the formula and essence of the fire suit where you need to take action and make a choice. You have two choices in front of you. What are those choices and which one will you make?

The Ace of Wands showed a positive indication of something having the potential to blossom and turn into more if you take action on it. The Two of Wands in a reading shows that extra promise. It says that any effort or action you put into now will bring about positive results. It's taking that effort even further than the idea. It's expanding that spark of passion you had for something or someone.

In the traditional image of the Two of Wands a human figure stands on the lookout. One hand holds onto a Wand and the other hand carries a globe. He has the world in his hands that says anything is possible. The hand holding onto one Wand shows that he is halfway to his destination. He is a visionary looking at all aspects of how to bring something to fruition. This can be saying that you are halfway to achieving the desire related to your question.

You've been putting in an effort and perhaps are unsure if it's worth it. The Two of Wands is reminder to keep moving forward and that you are heading in the right direction. You may need re-evaluate certain things, but you're on the right track. It can indicate partnerships of all types moving to the forefront. Someone around you that you know or will know soon will team up with you whether that's in a business pursuit or a love relationship. The partnership will be an exciting passionate and enthusiastic one regardless if it's business, love, friendship, or family. If you're asking about a new job, then this is a great card to receive showing that it's on the way.

Two of Wands in a reading says you've been making excellent progress surrounding the question you're asking. It can also indicate a courageous choice that needs to be made about something that will take you to the next plateau. This card's message says that you can do it. Be bold, be brave, be creative!

This points to someone who has the world in their hands, but there may be some discontentment about it. You need to take a step back and look at the bigger picture to decide what move should be made next.

This is also about choices and decisions to be made. Perhaps you want to buy a house and you have the money for it, but you're not doing anything to make it happen. You have the resources and you can afford it. You need to take action and make it happen. This scenario can be applied to most anything you're asking about.

If you're asking about a potential love interest, then this is saying take action and ask them out. Don't wait for them to make a move if they're not doing or saying anything. If they say no, then you'll have your answer sooner than later. This card is typically a positive one in that respect. It indicates strong passionate partnerships that gain confidence while in one another's presence.

Two of Wands can also be the opposite attracts card. It shows a strong partnership between two people who may be opposites of one another, but can go the distance when they use their strengths to contribute to an even bigger dynamic duo.

This indicates an excellent business partnership as both have something to offer what the other lacks. This might also be a pairing where one partner is extroverted and the other is introverted. Two of Wands is about making a choice and going for it. It tells you that the potential for a positive outcome is present, but you might not be helping it along. Whether this is resources, ideas, another person, or input. You already have what you need to make it happen, but you're not doing anything about it. This is telling you to make the next move.

You received the great career you always wanted and dreamed about, but you're not celebrating it. You're hesitant and taking a step back as if removed from it. It's like in the image of the Two of Wands where he stands strong and together with his head up in confidence looking out into the distance. It's the dreamer looking ahead as to what's next, but he hasn't quite made the move yet. This card shows that he's about to or it's telling him that he needs to.

Since Two of Wands is also the partnership card, it can be indicating that there is someone who shows up that is of benefit to your question. They may be someone who passes on words of wisdom that helps you in bringing the question to conclusion. It can be the author with a great idea, but this card is telling that person to sit down and write the book instead of thinking about it. This is a positive card that the book would be a success IF you write it. It can also indicate the author finds an agent or publisher, which is the positive merging of two energy forces. In the end, the Two of Wands is indicating that one takes action and goes for it to make something happen as you will succeed! You are halfway to your goal so keep going.

Three of Wands

*T*he Three of Wands is the visionary with clairvoyant foresight into what's coming up ahead. It can indicate travel, movement, or exploring areas of interest that you have yet to investigate. When you take a moment to step back and see what's coming up ahead, then you're able to act efficiently.

The Three of Wands can be telling you that your ship is coming in. What you've been on the lookout for is on its way if it's not yet present already. If you've been struggling with a work related endeavor, this card is a reminder to keep going as the rewards are on the horizon. There will be a positive pay off in the end. This is the same for a love reading with someone who is single. The Three of Wands says this person is on its way and will show up soon. You're at a place where you're ready and it will be happening.

With the Two of Wands card, the man in the image was holding a world globe in his hands and looking out into the horizon and seeing nothing there, but with the Three of Wands he's still looking out into the horizon, but this time he sees ships sailing towards him in the distance. The Three of Wands is a welcome relief card that your efforts have not gone unnoticed and positive blessings are heading towards you. This can be compensation for the idea you originally put into action. It can be the potential love interest heading towards you.

The Three of Wands is looking ahead to the future, whether that is a psychic premonition that comes to you, or a business CEO outlook where you take the long view on an issue. This card can be attributed to all of the visionaries of the world who opened doors for others. They are the ones setting the example and leading the pact.

The message can also be about going the distance whether it is with your career or relationship. This is taking it a step higher than where one's current position is. It shows longevity and promise. It can perhaps be a job promotion, a stronger commitment to a job role, or a new leadership stance at work. This can also be about planning ahead for your future. Implement steps that lead you towards the goal you desire.

This is also one of the travel cards. In a love reading, it can reveal that you come across a potential love partner while vacationing. Vacationing can also be a weekend getaway not too far from where you live. It can be taking additional vacation days off from work to have some time off allowing you to be out and about when you bump into this potential.

If you're already in a relationship, then this can show a strong passionate partnership where you work together on all aspects of your lives. This can also reveal a connection that is about to move to the next level of commitment. There will be a stronger bonding moment that deepens the connection. It can also be saying that you and your love mate should take some time off to spend with one another.

The Ace of Wands was the idea, the Two of Wands was putting that idea into action, and the Three of Wands is witnessing the beginning of the rewards filtering in from that action. Three of Wands typically reveals success on the horizon surrounding whatever the question was. Don't react to anything, but allow circumstances to evolve naturally.

Four of Wands

*T*he Four of Wands is a fantastic card to get on all levels and in all areas of one's life. It is one of my personal favorites in this suit. It implies that the solid security and foundation you desire is here now or is on its way. It's the completion of a creative project or work endeavor where abundance is inbound. It can be purchasing a new home or celebrating the success of something, whether it's a job offer or new love relationship.

This can be about celebrating how far you've come in some aspect of your life, including spiritually. It can be asking you to take time for yourself to do something fun, go out with a friend, or throw a party. The Four of Wands asks you to bask in your current blessings and enjoy what you have. Perhaps you entered into a new relationship or started a new job. This is about being in a place where you can relax as all is taken care of for you. This is one of the dreams come true messages associated with luxury.

In a love relationship, this can indicate a stronger commitment such as marriage, a wedding, proposals, or two people acknowledging they are in a long term relationship by having the talk. When wondering about a potential love partner, the Four of Wands can indicate the person is strong, secure, and stable. They are marriage material and seeking a long term love relationship.

The traditional image of this card shows two people hanging with each other outdoors with four wands forming a square around them. This symbolizes strong stability. This is a couple that is serious about each other and have plans to continue to grow and expand.

The Four of Wands can forecast that the love relationship coming in is the marriage or long term relationship partner. It would also show you two living together and creating a life with one another.

If you've been in an unhappy situation, the Four of Wands shows you breaking out of that and finding freedom where you're the one in control of you. In the end, the message with this card shows a period of uplifting joyful energy where everything feels wonderfully secure.

The Ace of Wands was the fantastic idea or prospect, the Two of Wands was putting that idea into action and taking it to the next level. The Three of Wands was perfecting that idea and noticing the beginnings of the rewards coming in as a result. The Four of Wands is the rewards and success has arrived and you may now celebrate! You've received what you desired, took action on, and now you're comfortable.

Five of Wands

*T*he Five of Wands message can reveal challenges, ego domination, corruption, or antagonism. You're in the midst of a rivalry with someone, or it's happening around you. The energy surrounding this card is uncomfortable, hostile, angry, and not usually pleasant. This can show two people or parties at odds with one another.

The Five of Wands causes all sorts of anxiety, sweats, tension, or anger. This can also be a warning to watch your back and steer clear of any drama swirling around you. This can ask you to step up to the plate and do damage control in a situation or circumstance.

In a love relationship, this can indicate discord, conflict, or arguments. I did a read once for someone where this card came up and the person being read for confirmed that their partner was constantly nit picking and bickering at them. It was troublesome for them to be on the receiving end of that energy.

The positive side to the Five of Wands is that it can be about healthy competition or passionate competitive energy. This can also be about friendly lively debate and communication. It can be about sports games, exercise training, or competitive fitness. Maybe you're heading to the beach or a park with some friends to play volleyball.

This card would indicate the day's energy as showing friendly competition.

In career or work related areas, this can show a temporary conflict or challenge that you need to overcome. This can also point to petty arguing or bickering. You would need to find middle ground, or compromise, and compassionate understanding in order to resolve conflict. Because this also points to opposing viewpoints, it can cause tiring disagreements where no one is listening to the other person. The overall energy of this card reveals someone to be absolved in unnecessary time wasting drama.

In the end, this card is not usually life threatening. It will blow over as long as you help move it along. You have to learn to let certain things go. Choose your battles wisely. The Five of Wands is representative of the world's typical energy which is usually ego based, challenging, and antagonistic to begin with. No one listens to opposing views or takes it to heart. Instead it's tons of angry reacting to another person. The Five of Wands would show this as being a petty time waster that helps no one in any form. It's wasted energy that could best be used for something more constructive.

The Five of Wands points to a challenge in your life or to watch your back as someone may be darting negativity at you. It reveals drama and discord. You may be mired down in negative bitter angry feelings. This can be temporary conflict or challenges that you need to overcome. This can also point to petty arguing or bickering, which is the opposite of compromise and compassionate resolving.

If every time you do a read over several months and this card keeps coming up, then you may want to evaluate your life and ways you can implement positive changes in order to move out of this challenging energy. The Five of Wands can make you feel as if you're in a battle every second.

Six of Wands

*T*he Six of Wands at its core is about achieving victory. The traditional image shows a warrior soldier riding a white steed into town. The crowds in the town surround him cheering exuberantly. He rides with his head up conveying independent, cocky, confidence. This can say that some form of public recognition is forthcoming. This is an especially great card for entrepreneurs or artists trying to sell their work. It reveals some measure of rising popularity.

The previous Five of Wands revealed challenges and struggle, but the Six of Wands shows you conquering those challenges riding sky high victorious. The Six of Wands points to awards, recognition, or positive praising words. This can also be showing you to have a sense of pride or an inflated ego. You know you're the bomb and are proud of it. This kind of big confidence can turn some people off who are threatened or insecure. The Six of Wands person doesn't care, pays no mind, and keeps focused on their goals and achievements. They are proud of themselves and have high self-esteem. They know their worth and aren't afraid to strut their stuff. Despite some seeing that as arrogance, it's not a bad thing to love yourself. The worst that comes out of that is it can rub some the wrong way. Having confidence is better than coming off like a victim.

This is a positive optimistic card that shows high self-confidence and knowing the good that you are and are deserving of. If you've been struggling to make something happen such as a project, getting into a relationship, buying a home, starting a business, or whatever it is, then this card shows that everything will end in your favor in bigger ways than you expect. You might even gloat about it. This can also indicate positive progress happening surrounding your goals.

In a love reading, this is an exciting message to receive. If you're asking about what someone thinks of you, then this might say that the person admires you. They may be putting you on a pedestal or have a high regard for you. The recognition in this sense is they may compliment you constantly through a date. If you have your eye on someone and you're hesitant to approaching them, then this says go for it as you will conquer their attention and they will be interested.

If you're asking about personality traits of someone, then the Six of Wands can be saying that the person has reached a high level of achieving. They might be in the public eye. You might not know who they are, but others who are fans around the world do. Perhaps they're a speaker, an author, teacher, social media sensation, or popular in their inner circle of friends and all those they come across. This is someone who is super confident and knows how great they are. The negative side is they might be too confident that it could exhaust someone with all of that me-me-me energy. In the end, this is someone to be admired on some level. They are certainly interesting and accomplished in some area or genre of their life.

In a love relationship, this can reveal a power couple. They're a dynamite connection that praises and admires one another. When they both join together, then there is nothing they cannot accomplish. They are winners that stop at nothing to achieve. They are popular and admired by those they come across. They might be low key, but when they go out, others see them as looking good together. They have a natural ease of comfortability and synastry that is witnessed and admired around them.

Seven of Wands

The Seven of Wands is about defending yourself or your position on a matter, value, or circumstance. This could reveal that there is someone who will attempt to confront you. Conjure up your strength and stand your ground, then you will conquer any challenges preventing you from winning or achieving your desires.

The typical image of the Seven of Wands shows a figure using a wand to attack six wands that appear to be attacking him, but the figure fights back with great confidence. The image is a positive one that he is overpowering the others who are attacking. This is a good card in the sense that one is taking down the bully or the lynch mob. The challenge of this card is that you have to gain the energy and strength to swat the flies away of the noise attacking you. The positive is that you can defeat them by staying true to yourself no matter what. This includes speaking your truth with assertiveness.

The Seven of Wands people are the movers and shakers of the world. This is someone who makes things happen. These are people who are not immune to controversy and keep their stance despite negative talk or bullying. They overcome and persevere as long as they stand strong. You may be the victim of negative talk or people criticizing or judging you. Pay no mind and stand in your power against this opposition. You are the light among the darkness of sharp critical tongues.

The Seven of Wands can also show an aggressive person who bulldozes to get their point across. Even if they're not being attacked or criticized, they have the stance as if they are. This is often how many behave on social media and comment boards over anything they disagree with. It is a warning to take it down a notch or relax if you are diving into the pit of gossip.

This can represent someone unwavering in their response or actions. They stand their ground and will not budge no matter how much someone persists. They are defiant and stubborn unwilling to back down or bend. This leads to conviction and can describe someone's character as having principle, which is a good quality to have. This can also be someone who is self-righteous, even if the majority disagree with them.

In a love reading, if you're single then this card might suggest that you're intending on obtaining a lover even if your life depends on it. The opposite extreme is that you're too defiant that it doesn't help others to warm up to you, including the right one. What does someone think of you? This suggests that they consider you to be independent and strong willed, which are good attracting qualities. The message with this card vacillates from something positive to challenging. This can be asking you to not give up on love or a potential love partner as there is a possibility of obtaining this person. In a love relationship, this might indicate that you and your partner have opposing views, or you feel as if you have to constantly defend yourself with them. This is not a particularly romantic card where love is concerned, but on the positive side it can reveal a couple who has an us against the world mentality.

The Five of Wands indicated a challenge you needed to overcome, while the Six of Wands had you conquering that challenge and winning, but the Seven of Wands reveals you to be on top. This will be met with naysayers and others attempting to bring you down. You are capable of facing this resistance head on. You may not enjoy fighting the mob off, but the Seven of Wands says that you will dominate and win.

Eight of Wands

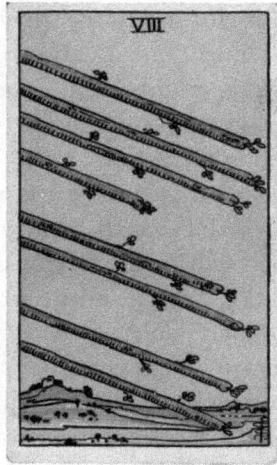

$\mathcal{T}$he Eight of Wands comes rushing in like eight missiles shooting rapidly across the sky. This card points to fast movement or change of some kind. Any surrounding cards can determine what this fast movement is about if it's unclear. If there are positive cards then this can say that what you desire is coming into your vicinity soon and quickly, but if it's challenging, then this might indicate some speed bumps heading in. This card can also represent travel, typically by air, but not always.

The Eight of Wands is a card that points to rapid ambition. This is someone climbing the ladder of success quickly. There is no stopping this person as they glide upwards to the top. If one has been experiencing no movement on anything for some time, then the Eight of Wands is a welcome relief that what you desire is coming in fast, instantaneously, and out of the blue. It can also show someone who is working quite a bit diving into various activities and projects. This is not someone sitting idly waiting for something to happen. They are going out there, nabbing it, and getting it. There is nothing standing in your way to grab what you desire.

This is typically a positive yes card to the question being asked. You want to know if you should apply for that job or ask that person out on a date, then this card is saying yes go for it now!

The Eight of Wands also suggests you're wrapping up final loose ends on a situation or circumstance. If it's a general question then this can be about important information, news, or messages being announced in your favor. This is about circumstances moving hurriedly into your life. You might be busy juggling all sorts of things at the same time, but this is exhausting energy. The energy of this card is an upbeat, exciting, and lively energy.

The Eight of Wands card is one of the rare cards in the Minor Arcana set of the Traditional Tarot that have no people in it. If you were constantly being met with one roadblock after another, then this message shows that the coast is clear. Be prepared for quick active motion with nothing to block you from what you're aiming for. This is also the success card on whatever the question is surrounding. Buying that car or home, accepting that new job or relationship. This is quick action resolving all challenges as you fly forward full speed ahead.

If you're single and asking if there will be a new love, then this card says yes this potential is coming quickly and things will happen rapidly without effort or worry. It's like a shot gun connection where the two meet and instantly feel a mutual spark as if they've already known each other before. If one is already in a love relationship, then this indicates smooth sailing up ahead. With the Eight of Wands, one doesn't necessarily need to do much as the energy carries them forward immediately. This is the card of expecting the unexpected in a good way, unless the cards following it are challenging, then this shows rapid movement towards challenges.

If one is looking to find personality traits of an incoming partner, then the Eight of Wands can show that the person is a busy person leading a fast paced life. They are enthusiastic, energetic, and active. They might be a heavy traveler or always in motion and on the go. If you prefer quiet and calm, then this potential might not be welcoming or you'll have to accept that opposites attract and that this is how this person is. Sometimes a quiet and calm person prefers someone who is always on the go, while the on the go fast paced person welcomes the quiet and calm person to balance them out.

Nine of Wands

At the end of the movie "Thelma and Louise", the Louise character says, "I'm not giving up." The Thelma character says, "Let's keep going." This is the theme of the Nine of Wands card. It says you've been weary from constant battle, but it's asking you not to give up. Keep going as you're closer than you think to your goal. It's the card of persevering even though you might be exhausted.

The differences between the Nine of Wands and the Seven of Wands is that with the Seven of Wands you were energetic and fending off all your opponents with enthusiasm, but the Nine of Wands is that you're exhausted, but still pushing through. It's giving until it hurts, and then you give more.

The energy of this card is that you've been losing a battle and everyone knows you're losing, yet you keep going as far as you can go regardless. Political candidates running for office or sports players have the energy of this card at times. They might be falling behind or stand no chance at winning, yet they keep going as far as they can go, and end up making it! Often times, the Nine of Wands can show you winning, but not without a fight.

The Seven of Wands shows the figure in the image fighting others off, while the Nine of Wands shows the figure standing strong ready to go to battle with the wands all upright, except that he might not necessarily be in battle the way the Seven of Wands is. The Nine of Wands is on the defensive, while the Seven of Wands is striking back. The Nine of Wands is primed to strike back as evident of his face, but he stands on guard as if he might have to. This may also show someone who has no reason to be on the defensive, but they're overall disposition is one feeling as if they are in fighting mode.

The Nine of Wands in a reading can mean that you or someone has the stance of feeling as if you'll need to fight back on a circumstance, even if you don't technically need to fight back. There is something in you that feels as if you have to. This is someone who is on the defensive. Others might say, "Calm down, I'm on your side."

Wands are of the element of fire, so when the Wands is angry they can hold a grudge like nobody's business. The Nine of Wands can be about someone who is self-preserved or self-protecting and on high alert. When something happens in someone's life that bothers them, they might vent with friends or put up a post on social media ranting about what someone did or how over it they are. This points to the Nine of Wands energy. Circumstances might be fine in truth, but you feel as if you've been dragged through the ringer clawing, kicking, and fighting back. Now you're standing there holding the Wand almost leaning on it angrily looking around to see if anyone is going to try and take a piece of you.

The Nine of Wands is the card of the warrior or a soldier primed to go to battle. In a reading, this can be that you're being paranoid about someone who is back in your life again after they previously betrayed your heart. It might be an ex-lover who did you wrong, then you broke up, and they're back with you again. The Nine of Wands can show you to be feeling paranoid that they might do something that negatively affects you again.

This card can be telling you to keep going with a project or a job where you're ready to throw in the towel. It can also be saying that your paranoid feelings are not unfounded and to continue to watch your back around someone. The Nine of Wands is a reminder that you've come so far, keep going, you can do it!!

In a love reading for someone single asking about a potential's personality, this can show that person as having tremendous strength no matter what. You don't want to cross this person negatively as they will attack. They might appear hard and rough around the edges, but this is because life may have made them this way. If you look deeper, you'll find a trusted friend who has your back and will go to battle with or for you.

If you're single and asking about love, then this card can be asking you to not give up and keep searching. This can reveal that you've been frustrated and over it, but the Nine of Wands says that love is coming, so keep the faith and persevere. The Nine of Wands can be the opposite of that where it's saying that you appear to be standoffish and defensive. This is not welcoming potentials into your environment. You would need to evaluate if you need to make changes or not with how you appear to others by being softer, kinder, and friendly.

If you're already in a love relationship, then this may be a challenging card to receive. It can say that you or your partner are defensive with one another. It's as if you feel they're constantly criticizing or attacking your every move. You are on the defensive even though they may have stopped criticizing, but the scars are still there. This would be a warning card to ease the mind of one another. Sometimes no problems are evident in a relationship, but one of the partners feels defensive for reasons you cannot figure out. This is someone ready to go to battle, even though there is no reason to be.

In the movie, "I Am Sam", the Rita character is a good example of the Nine of Wands energy. Someone who is ready for battle. She answers her phone and it's her estranged husband asking how she is. With hostility she insists she's fine, but responds again, "What do you mean what do I mean by that?!" You constantly feel as if you're tip-toing around your partner because they're touchy about every little thing you say or do. This is someone tense and on guard.

This card can continue to show up for a couple who have surpassed their expiration date. It's a never ending cycle of feeling a hostility or defensiveness with the other partner even though they're not doing or saying anything wrong. While the Five of Wands would show a constant struggle in motion, the Nine of Wands is feeling as if there is a constant struggle. This may ask you both to lighten up, put down the wall, and meet one another half way.

Ten of Wands

*T*he Ten of Wands shows you carrying too much weight on your shoulders. You may have overextended yourself in all areas of your life and you need to make some healthy life changes. This might be the person juggling too much work and not incorporating enough rest and relaxation. It will catch up with you if you don't do something about it.

The image in the traditional Ten of Wands shows someone carrying all ten wands on their hunched over back struggling to carry them on their journey. The goal they want to achieve is in sight if they can just get up that hill. They're already exhausted and still pushing themselves beyond what is considered healthy. Therefore, they may not be able to make it if they continue. This is the card telling someone to take some time off! You are taking on way too much. The previous Nine of Wands showed you to be exhausted and primed for battle, but the Ten of Wands says you are no longer primed for battle, you're just plain worn out and cannot make it, but are insisting on pushing.

The message in the Ten of Wands can be asking you to lighten the load or delegate to others. While it is possible one can make it to their destination in this state, it won't be met without exhaustion. There are repercussions involved with the Ten of Wands at times. This is also the physical exhaustion card. You're using up too much physical energy that it will catch up with you. This can be someone who comes home from work and always says, "I'm so tired." Those who are in the full time work force or corporate worlds working for someone else may see this card appear for them. The current five days a week break your back work is no longer conducive to the positive well-being of one's self. There isn't enough time off and this is causing health issues, permanent unhappiness, stress, and other physical detriments. Many don't take enough time off or they feel guilty about using their vacation days. The Ten of Wands is saying, "You've pushed yourself too hard and it's time to take a little break." You need to start thinking of you when this card comes up.

This message can also be saying that you're not saying no to someone when you really want to. You're taking on what others are giving or telling you while carrying the weight of that burden. This can be a card that illustrates you have to do damage control surrounding an issue. This is someone who makes things harder than it has to be. There is no method to their madness. They do things in ways that don't make much sense and seem to be the unnecessary hard way.

This can also be about someone who is working so hard on something, but isn't witnessing that much return. It can be a blessing in disguise if there is a Ten of Pentacles card in the spread, then this might suggest that you have been working so hard for so long, and the Ten of Pentacles shows you will reap positive rewards. It's not much further now even though you will be exhausted over the efforts. However, if it's next to the Five of Pentacles, then it might indicate a loss after all this hard work for nothing.

In a love relationship, this might say that you're working way too hard leaving you exhausted to the point where you're neglecting your partner or personal life. This card could also indicate that you or your partner feels burdened by the relationship. It's no longer loving or fun. It might be that you or your partner is constantly doing things to keep the relationship going positively or that you're always the one taking care of things. This soon starts to feel as if you're being taking advantage of and that you have to carry all the weight. This same concept can be applied in other areas such as with career and work life too. The message with these challenging cards or meanings is to take action steps to correct this behavior so that you're happier and less burdensome.

If you're single and looking, then this card might suggest that you're too busy in your day to day life that there is no room to invite in a partner for a relationship. When would you see them? Modifications would need to be made to your personal life too. The Ten of Wands says that you're pushing so hard to find a romantic partner that it's wearing you out leaving you in constant frustration ready to throw in the towel.

Page of Wands

PAGE of WANDS.

PERSON:

The Page of Wands can reveal a young person under or around the age of 25 who has a Fire sign in the top tier of their chart. This is Aries, Leo, Sagittarius. *(Top tier can be Sun sign, Rising, Moon, Venus, Mars.)*

If they do not have those stats, then this is someone regardless of age or sign who is restless, impulsive, extroverted, excited, and always on the go. When this young passionate person comes racing in, they just as quickly race out. They are the most impulsive and reckless of all the Pages. Bursting with energy they grow bored if a relationship or endeavor is not exciting and interesting around the clock. This Page doesn't need to be told they're great. They have natural confidence and already know it.

The flipside is the Page of Wands person can be too confident and a know it all who speaks out of turn. They're the ones in the classroom who call out without raising their hand. Their passionate forthright energy can be infectious and therefore they are naturally popular. This is a charming being who enjoys attention, but can be prone to moodiness on occasion. This person also may have tons of pride, so it could take them awhile to apologize for something, or they'll apologize right away just to keep things moving along. The Page of Wands character is a free spirit running from place to place. They can be impatient and out the door without apology. Where the Page of Pentacles prefers to be around one or two close friends at a time, the Page of Wands loves to be surrounded by a big social circle.

MESSENGER:

The answer to a question with this card can be a resounding yes. Will the person contact me? Yes, but it may be a superficial message of attraction, desire, and passion. This person might send a hot racy text, email, or phone call. They require your immediate attention and will keep persisting frantically until they give up and move onto something or someone else just as quickly. The Page of Wands blows in and out fast. What they desire today can change tomorrow. This is why this can be a superficial message. On a more serious work related note, the message of the Page of Wands can be an answered prayer or good news related to a job offer, promotion, or work related project. It'll come through via any means possible such as post office mail, email, text, phone call, or social media message.

SITUATION:

The Page of Wands as a situation in a reading can read much like the Ace of Wands where this is the start or a spark of a new creative endeavor. It can be that you need to be impulsive about a situation and act quickly. This is someone filled with ideas and excitement. This is not a planner, but someone who dives head on into things. Caution should be adhered to when you're in an impulsive mood. Weigh the consequences and pros and cons before jumping in blindly. At the same time the Page of Wands can be telling you to take that risk. Be passionate and fearless and go after what you want with gusto. Be a natural born confident leader.

This is about taking action on something. Coming up with an idea and getting to work on it. This card can bring inspiration whether divinely guided or inspiration from another person. If you have reservations about something, then this says to remove those doubts and fears and do it. The Page of Wands doesn't think about or entertain the word fear. If this Page wants something, it goes out and gets it without reservation.

The Page of Wands can also indicate travel, taking a vacation, or movement with something including your body in physical exercise. The Page of Wands can be the start of a passionate relationship that may be fiery and intense, but could fizzle out quickly.

Knight of Wands

KNIGHT of WANDS.

PERSON:

The Knight of Wands can reveal a person around 25-35 who has a Fire sign in the top tier of their chart. This is Aries, Leo, Sagittarius. *(Top tier can be Sun sign, Rising, Moon, Venus, Mars)*

If they do not have those stats, then this is someone regardless of age or sign who is a thrill and adventure seeker. They love the outdoors and competitive sports. Sitting around doing nothing will drive them crazy. They need to have their body moving with quick active speed. This is a dynamic go getter personality. They are more likely the one to make the first move. This is a confident person who holds their head up high. They race into a party and everyone gets excited and crowds around them. They are super popular enjoying the attention, but due to their restless energy they quickly gallop out of there since they can't be in one place for too long.

The Knight of Wands person can be exceedingly charming. They're not afraid to ask for what they want. Sometimes they might come off too pushy, but they carry a winning smile or charming attitude that seduces others into bowing to their whim. This is a very self-confident person that can border on cockiness at times. It may exhaust others listening to the Knight of Wands constantly telling you how great they are. We know they're great, but don't need to hear it around the clock. On the flipside this kind of confidence and high self-esteem can rub off positively on others. It motivates you to try harder, measure up, and feel good about yourself.

This person is an explorer always seeking out new opportunities and circumstances to investigate and dive into. The Knight of Wands knows they are the bomb. This energy pulls you out of the funk if you've been down for some time. They're the friend you want to go out with to be cheered up.

SITUATION:

The Knight of Wands tells you to seize the opportunity! Don't waste another minute and go after what you want. This is also the card of sexual passionate attraction. The one you have your eye on may or may not be in love with you, but they are definitely physically attracted to you. Be careful if it's love you're after with this person as the Knight of Wands can indicate a fleeting booty call or sexual escapade. Look to other deeper commitment oriented romantic cards in the spread to see if there is the potential for more or if there is love. This person is in lust with you, but this is not to be confused with love.

This can also suggest some form of travel is about to happen in your life. It can be asking you to make a move on something you desire without haste. It may imply that you've been restless lately and need to channel that into something productive.

The Knight of Wands in a situation reading can be asking you to believe in yourself knowing you can do it. It's about being innovative, creative, and daring. In a love reading, it can show a love potential coming in. It will be a fun passionate relationship where you both enjoy one another, spending time together, exploring adventures, places, and heading on little trips. If you're single and wondering where you'll bump into this person, the Knight of Wands shows a social event, occasion, or a place of physical activity such as hiking, or the gym.

Queen of Wands

QUEEN of WANDS.

PERSON:

The Queen of Wands can reveal a person around aged 35 and above who has a Fire sign in the top tier of their chart. This is Aries, Leo, Sagittarius. *(Top tier can be Sun sign, Rising, Moon, Venus, Mars)*

If they do not have those stats, then this is someone regardless of age or sign who is charismatic, a doer, passionate, and highly sociable. This is a person who is typically outgoing and upbeat. They walk in a room and all eyes are on them. They radiate a sunshine energy that seems to infect all those it comes across. No party should be without a Queen of Wands person.

The Queen of Wands is usually the host/hostess throwing the party and putting it together. Once they've organized the whole thing, they're the ones who cheerily enter the party greeting every single person with a hello hug and handshake. The smile is constantly plastered and genuine to the max. There is no pretense with this person. The Queen of Wands loves seeing everyone together having a good time. This person may have a career, family, home, and still manage to have a personal life. You rarely see this person sitting around idly doing nothing. They exude sunshine and positive energy in whichever direction they point their eyes.

Like all of the Queens in the Tarot, this person is independent and strong able to create striking advances with subtle movements. The Queen of Wands is no exception, but is the loudest of all Queens. This person expects the best and wants everyone to participate.

The Queen of Wands can be over controlling and demanding at times. When things don't go their way they can get moody, but it's not the quiet withdrawn moodiness. They let their moodiness shine out in ways such as being overly critical and harsh, but when they calm down they end up making it up to the person in magnificently deep ways that the person on the receiving end lets it go. It's difficult to stay mad at the Queen of Wands because the energy of this person is infectious on a good day. They have a perfectionist attitude and want everything to be just right. This is someone with constant energy, and even when they're tired, they keep going with gusto.

SITUATION:

The Queen of Wands in a general reading can be telling you to go after what you want. Let yourself soar to greater heights. Be the leader you were born to be. It can also be asking you to make sure that you've got balance in your life. The Queen of Wands can show someone who is always on the go, busy working, and creating. A balance may need to be brought in so that you also have some measure of a personal life. Or it might be saying that you're having too much fun and need to get to work!

This is about being driven and making what you want happen through action. Have self-confidence and the right cheery attitude with all endeavors you partake in from work related projects to love relationships. This can also be to take care of yourself physically as the Queen of Wands is into physical fitness and radiates this vibrant nature.

In a love reading, this can show someone as being loyal, adventurous, and passionate. They bring out the best in you and in others. If you're single, it can either suggest you'll meet someone that fits the general description of the Queen of Wands, or it's asking you to get out there and mingle as the Queen of Wands would do. Get out there and let yourself be seen. Don't shy away from potentials, but instead approach them with a warm smile. The Queen of Wands is not shy. When this person likes someone, they tell that person and the world. They shout it from the rooftops. Relationships here are usually passionate and fiery. It's a couple who is on an equal playing field contributing equal amounts to a relationship if not more. This card may also warn against being the victim of your own ego. The Queen of Wands can be prone to tantrums when they don't get their way.

King of Wands

KING of WANDS

PERSON:

The King of Wands can reveal a person around aged 35 and above who has a Fire sign in the top tier of their chart. This is Aries, Leo, Sagittarius. *(Top tier can be Sun sign, Rising, Moon, Venus, Mars)*

If they do not have those stats, then this is someone regardless of age or sign who is passionate, a leader, charming, outgoing, charismatic, or a master at whatever they dive into.

This person has a fiery personality. When you're involved with someone like this, then expect to be on the constant go. You want to stay in and lounge on the couch? Too bad. The King of Wands says he's coming over to pick you up and you're going out whether you want to or not. Be prepared and ready to do so. This is a dashing whirlwind personality that knows he's the best. He is cocky and loves being worshipped and the center of the world's attention. He's an entrepreneur accomplishing all that he envisions. He may work all day, but then he's ready to play afterwards. He has boundless energy at his fingertips. This is a super confident and outgoing person.

The negatives or challenges is this person has a bigger ego than most and quite a bit of pride. They can be prone to egocentricity, narcissism, and selfishness. Yet, in a love connection they have a tendency to also share, rave, and boast about their admiration for you. This is someone who would make a great agent constantly raving about their client in wordy descriptive ways. They love showing off about themselves, but also showing off their love partner and friends. This is a loud upbeat person who knows how to make an entrance. When you need cheering up, this is the person that knows how to do it.

This is a risk taker and an entrepreneur who is fearless when it comes to success or failure. They're always on the go and not one to be confined at home for all eternity. If you're involved with a King of Wands, then you'll need to allow them freedom of movement to come and go on their adventures. They might come home one day to announce they're going on a sabbatical for a week to Africa....alone. Don't take it personally and allow them that independence, otherwise if they feel the restraints are too tight, they'll be off in search of another land to start new roots. They like a little possession as they equate that to loyalty and admiration, but just as long as their chains don't keep them homebound permanently. This guy/girl is also into sports or physical activity of some kind. They need to be physical or they go crazy.

SITUATION:

The King of Wands in a general situation reading can indicate achievement and success. This is about being your most magnificent confident self. Going after what you want and obtaining it. This is about focusing on your desires and removing all distractions in order to obtain and accomplish that. Do whatever needs to be done to achieve whatever it is you're after. The King of Wands shows that you will get it as long as you remain vigilant.

This is also a creative card that asks you to be innovative, inspiring, and original. With the King of Wands, you are asked to be confident, fearless, outgoing, and a strong composed leader. Take charge of what you desire and make it happen.

In a love relationship reading, this can show a super passionate person or couple. It is an incredibly fiery duo who is loyal and worshipping of one another, but fiery passion can also bring on jealous rages and dramatic arguments. This couple is so consumed by one another that they don't allow the occasional rift to ruin their love. They are the kind of couple who have tons of make-up sex.

The King of Wands can reveal a couple who both go out of their way to please one another. This can be by showering each other with gifts, praises, or massages. They enjoy moving and traveling around sometimes together and other times alone. As dependent as they might be on one another overall, they take regular time outs of doing their own thing separately. Neither are bothered by that in the slightest. They have passion for their careers or work, but this is never an issue because of this similarity. They're on the same page and this makes it a dynamic easygoing connection. They're an adventurous passionate couple who are the talk of the town.

Swords/Air

*T*he Swords suit resides in the element of air. Astrologically it can represent the signs of Gemini, Libra, Aquarius.

The Swords suit in the Tarot tend to contain more challenging cards than any of the other Minor Arcana elements. The Swords/Air element represents ones thinking, mental, and communicative processes. Most of the challenges and chaos created by human souls are generated from the mind, so it's no surprise that the Swords suit is bathed in challenges.

Challenges are not necessarily a bad thing. Lessons are born out of challenges. You learn and grow from them. The Swords suit helps you cut right to the heart of the matter allowing you a glimpse at what can be causing you heartache or issues.

The Swords/Air suit is associated with communication, mental processes, non-emotional personalities, analytical, reasoning, intellectual, wordy, conversational, probing, debating, thoughts, detachment, truth, ideas, thinking, or logic.

Ace of Swords

*T*he Ace of Swords is the card of clarity. This is someone whose mental acumen and perception is crystal clear. When the Ace of Swords card shows up in a reading, then it might be saying that you already know the truth, or that the truth will be revealed. There will be no sugar coating it, but it will be as blunt as you can imagine. The truth revealed can be a blessing or challenge, regardless if it comes out in a direct or harsh way.

The Ace of Swords is about triumphing or conquering something. It is asking you to be direct, exact, and truthful. This is one of the more positive cards in the typically challenging Swords suit. The Ace of Swords asks you to be brave and have courage surrounding whatever the question is. It may also be asking you to be objective about a situation, which means you remain neutral and don't take a side. You hear both sides and understand where the other person is coming from without judgement or reaction.

The Ace of Swords is not intuitive since the Swords suit is lacking in feeling or emotion. It is analytical using logic, with mind over heart. It says its truth without any room for emotional blackmail.

This card may also ask you to analyze a situation in a deeper way to get to the heart of the matter. This would make a great message for someone who holds the stature of a judge, mediator, or balanced journalist who never seems to take anyone's side, but allows everyone to tell their story.

The Ace of Swords would also be a card to represent someone who is a part of the U.S. Independent Party. In America's current political climate, people have been trained to be either a Democrat or Republican, and then rigidly stay on the opposite ends without ever approving of anything anyone in either party say. While someone who is an Independent remains neutral in the middle without ever joining either side. They hear both sides of the parties' truth and then will decide what is a more justly cause to support. This is the Ace of Swords energy. Listening to all sides of someone and taking a balanced stance.

In a love reading, you ask about a potential lover and how they feel about you. This card might be saying that the truth will come out. Perhaps they have the talk with you that says they're not looking to get into a relationship with anyone right now, or they tell you they are interested in you. The Ace of Swords would show up to indicate someone coming forward with a piece of truth. It's the card that says the answer to your question is forthcoming. The response you receive from this other person will clear away any doubts even if it's something you don't want to hear. The truth is precise and to the point that there is no room for doubt, and then you can choose to put the issue to rest as it's resolved.

The Ace of Swords uses its sword to cut away any toxins or debris in the way from allowing one to get to the truth. This is the same case in love readings. If you're single and asking about a potential's personality traits, then this can reveal the person to be communicative. They are someone who operates on an intellectual level rather than the heart. They might be a writer or a chatty person who engages in lively debates with others. They might be someone who is a truth seeker or philosopher.

The Ace of Swords in relationships, whether single or involved with someone, is coming to the truth of a matter. It can be a passing thought that enters your mind that seems to fall into you from the Divine above. This truth or idea is the answered prayer or missing information piece you were wondering about. On a challenging note, this card can describe someone who is blunt, direct, and authoritarian.

The High Priestess or The Moon card might suggest information you're looking for is coming to you through your senses, heart, and Clairsentience (feeling) psychic channel. However, the Ace of Swords would show the information you're looking for is coming through your Claircognizance (thinking) channel. Therefore, with the Ace of Swords pay attention to your thoughts at this time to see what is a repetitive message, but is not coming from your ego.

You're going on a date with someone and wondering how it'll go. The Ace of Swords shows that it will go well where there is a meeting of the minds so to speak. You'll both deeply enjoy your lively banter conversation and in connecting mentally. In the end, this is what will give a clue to longevity since it's how you get along on a mental level rather than the physical attraction level that ensures you can both go the distance. Physical attraction isn't lasting and nor does it keep someone interested if you can't share ideas and thoughts. This is why the Ace of Swords can be a positive card to receive in terms of love.

The Ace of Swords is being a visionary and having a crystal clear channel with the other side in order to create striking work. In the traditional image of the Tarot you see a huge Sword being held by a hand pushed through a cloud. The cloud represents confusion and fog, but the sword piercing through it indicates cutting through the bull and seeing the truth of a situation. There is no confusion with the Ace of Swords since everything is crystal clear.

How does someone feel about you? The Ace of Swords shows this person thinking about you on some level, but this does not automatically equate to feelings. The Swords suit is ruled by thoughts, and in this case, they are having positive thoughts about you.

Two of Swords

*T*he Two of Swords shows a moment of pause before a decision or choice is about to be made or needs to be made. This is also a reminder that doing nothing and making no decision IS a decision. This might be suggesting that you need to make a decision about something, but are fearful of doing so. You're confused as you don't know which choice to make, or are afraid that it might be the wrong decision.

If you are unhappy at your job or you have periods where you want out, but are afraid to leave or make a move, then this would reveal that inner tug of war. This can apply to most any decision that needs to be made. It can be something minor such as you and a partner are going away for the weekend, but you both have been vacillating between indecision on where to go or where to stay while away.

This points to indecisiveness or being at a stalemate. It usually points to conflicted feelings unable to make a decision about something. The choice is great enough that it's keeping you from moving forward with anything else. You're stuck on the decision to make and don't know what to do or choose, but you do have to make a decision. Until you do, the energy will grow blocked preventing the ebb and flow of abundantly joyful life happening. You will get unstuck when you make a choice.

In a love reading, this can show the message of, "Should I stay or should I go?" You're all over the place in not knowing what to do. Part of you wants to leave, but the other part wants to stay. This can also be a message about the object of your desire. The Two of Swords is in conflict between heart and mind, but because it's the element of air, the mind tends to dominate. This goes against the true message of this guidance, which is follow your heart in the end because the mind changes when the ego is involved, but the heart goes on.

If you're in a relationship, you could be having a disagreement with the one you're with. This doesn't necessarily mean a fight. It could be a minor decision that needs to be made. You both have differing opinions or neither of you are making any choice at all. This can also be that you're bothered by something, but your partner isn't. Your partner is completely unaware of your inner turmoil over an issue. The Two of Swords indicates this opposing stance. This is also about not seeing the truth in front of you.

If there is someone you have a mutual crush on, then this can show that you're both waiting for the other one to make the move. You can move out of the mud you're stuck in when you make a decision to unlock this standoff. If you approach your crush and express your feelings, then you could find that you two grow closer afterwards. Get over the fear, bite the bullet, and take immediate action. There's no escaping the fact that you will have to choose. Everything will be more peaceful afterwards once you make a choice. Otherwise it prolongs the mental battle of indecision preventing anything else from occurring.

In love, you could be running around in circles with a love partner who doesn't seem to know what they want. You're sure they are into you and love you, but there are other signs that show otherwise causing you confusion.

This can show someone keeping you at arm's length where they never fully go away, but they don't stay either. They don't reveal their true feelings, which leads you to feel puzzled about how they feel. They could be feeling stuck not knowing whether to admit their feelings. Part of them may not want to be in the connection, but the other part of them does. This is a horrible space to be in for all involved, including the one experiencing this stuck in the mud space. This reveals a stubborn person refusing to make a decision. This hardens the energy preventing two people from moving on in their life. There could be other factors they've considered that prevent a decision from being made.

If you're single and dating around, then this might show several dating prospects where you're not fully sure about any of them. You're not feeling that 100% magic with any of the choices in front of you. Either stop dating around or hone in on the one you have your eye on most and develop that connection.

The traditional image of the Two of Swords shows a figure with two swords crisscrossing over her heart. This points to someone who is not revealing their feelings or intentions regardless if it is good or bad. This person also has a blindfold over her eyes which could mean you're not seeing the truth. This blinded truth and wall around your heart is preventing you from moving forward. Her back is to the water in the background which symbolizes your feelings. You are not facing your feelings or admitting them.

Not seeing the truth can indicate that you're living in denial about something. You might have an attraction to someone and be under the delusion that the one you like shares the same feelings. You refuse to see the truth that this person is not that interested. The Two of Swords can reveal all of these example cases. Sometimes when a relationship ends and one of the two people is heartbrokenly shocked, they might later say, "In hindsight, now that I look back on the connection there were red flags, but I chose to ignore them."

The Two of Swords would indicate that this person were refusing to see the truth and the signs, because they subconsciously didn't want it to be true. If they had a reading and this card came up, it would warn them about this reality. The Two of Swords is one of those challenges that goes away once you make the decision you're wrestling with. The point is that you're struggling with a decision, and the card message is telling you to follow your heart on this one, rather than talking yourself in or out of something.

Three of Swords

The Three of Swords can reveal some measure of suffering. It usually shows an image of three swords piercing into a heart. It doesn't get any clearer than that in symbolism.

When this card shows up in a reading, it's not generally welcomed with glee. It can be implying that you're about to find out a truth you may not want to hear or one that may cause some upset. It can be discovering that you didn't get the job you wanted, or that you lost the job you loved working at. It can be finding out that the person you've been dating has left you or no longer loves you. This can also reveal a circumstance that comes and goes quickly, but gives you a challenging day.

You've been thinking about leaving your job for some time, but you never do it and instead remain miserable at it. This is causing you prolonged turmoil. This card message is reminding you that you do not want to remain in this heartbreaking state forever and you need to do something to change that. Accept the job and make the most of it, or take actions steps to plan your exit safely.

I've heard others who are experiencing personal life pain say, "My heart hurts." The Three of Swords can show up in a reading to indicate that kind of heart wrenching pain.

In a love relationship reading, the Three of Swords can indicate upset, anxiety, or heartbreak. It shows up to reveal that a love relationship might be ending. Any heartbreak resulted out of the Three of Swords is temporary, but life in general is full of temporaries since nothing stays the same.

The message of this card can also show a couple going through a separation. The separation might be permanent, or it can be two people temporarily separated by distance. This is where one of them is travelling, or they moved further away from you. You can also live with them and still feel this distance as if you've both been disconnected from one another causing you pain. This can also indicate a long distance relationship, which is always challenging. This card can reveal a betrayal where someone turns against you causing you to silently suffer or internalize this pain.

The Three of Swords can reveal you to be experiencing loneliness or as if you're cut off from everything and in isolation. This is a card that reveals some kind of a feeling connected to emotional loss or you're feeling somber and melancholy. It is one of the more emotional cards in the Swords suit, which is unusual in the element of air. This is because the emotional loss felt here is connected to the mind. The feeling of loneliness due to not seeing your love partner can be altered by adjusting your thoughts into a space where you accept that it's temporary. Avoid focusing on pessimism and allow yourself to move through any pain and look at the brighter side of things.

The Three of Swords can reveal the end of a relationship, especially if one sees the card in the future position. This can also be that your love partner wants a temporary break or is busy travelling so much that you hardly see them. If it's in the future position it can show the pain of that separation enduring. There are people who get upset and hyper emotional when they don't see the person they're dating for a week. This card could show up to indicate this in a reading. The person is unnecessarily creating emotional drama in their mind that it's not okay to go a week and not see the person they're dating. Either way the Three of Swords ultimately reveals someone going through some measure of painful difficulty.

If you're single and asking about love, then this card can show that you're struggling with trying to find a partner. The lack of having a love partner is making you unhappy as if something is missing in your life. The Three of Swords might show that there is a love partner coming to you, but you're both currently separated for a period of time before they finally show up.

The Three of Swords can show emotional pain, but it also might be the result of hearing words you do not want to hear. It might have been from an argument. It can be that someone you love said something to you that wasn't kind. This includes a name calling situation or they relayed upsetting words to you such as that they don't want to be in a relationship anymore. The emotional upset can be over words unsaid that you picked up telepathically. Perhaps your love partner is ignoring you or not paying much attention to you. This puts you in a painful state as if they broke up with you. All of this could point to the pain associated with the Three of Swords.

Four of Swords

*T*he Four of Swords in a reading can be about quieting your mind from exhaustion and taking a break. This is the rest and relaxation recommended card. Perhaps you've been overworked pushing yourself to the extreme, then this is the message that it's time to put that all to rest and take a break. Go on a mini-weekend getaway to relax or quiet your mind in still peacefulness at home. Put aside pending issues that can wait. Cancel and change appointments if necessary.

The Four of Swords is also the meditation card. Typically, it shows an image of someone laying down at peace with their eyes closed. If you've been searching for answers about something, then this card can be recommending that you put that out of your mind for now as you're too clouded to reach a clear answer. Taking a break from the issue can bring about the guidance that can assist you.

You have been going to battle on a daily basis. This is wearing you out creating a thick fog around you. The Four of Swords shows up to indicate that it's time to take a break from it all and recharge your batteries.

This can also be that you have a choice or decision to make, but you're not making a decision yet. You're taking a few days to think about it. This isn't the same as the Two of Swords which indicates a struggle with making a decision, or a tug of war between heart and mind. The Four of Swords isn't necessarily a choice, but points to someone taking a break from making any decisions in order to gain additional insight and clarity by taking a time out.

In a love reading, this can imply that a temporary break or split is on the horizon. The difference between a split or break with the Four of Swords and the Three of Swords, is that the Three of Swords is a painful split or separation. The Four of Swords is a peaceful break such as you both live in separate places and have been spending quite a bit of time with one another. Now you're both choosing to spend a week apart in your own places for some time alone, which doesn't mean the relationship is over. You're both just busy with your personal activities while still communicating. The Four of Swords implies a temporary break from being in front of one another every second. This assists in the longevity of the relationship. It's not a painful separation, but a welcomed one on both ends. If it is a break up, then it's a mutually amicable peaceful one where neither of you have any interest in the other, so there is no pain involved.

The Four of Swords in a general read can be telling someone that they need to take a break from whatever the question is, whether it's a love relationship or a career choice. This card asks someone to sleep on it for now. Detach yourself from what to do at this point. When you re-emerge from this time out, then what's intended to happen will be. This would also be a common card to pull during the planetary Mercury Retrograde transit. Run an online search on the Mercury Retrograde and when it is if you haven't heard of it. The Mercury Retrograde transit happens three times a year where you're prompted to take pause and not act on anything or make any major decisions for a few weeks.

The generic terms associated with the Four of Swords are meditation, rest, relaxation, a time out, a break, a mini-vacation, seclusion, rest before the battle, or re-charge.

Five of Swords

$\mathcal{T}$he Five of Swords in a reading can reveal someone who initiated a battle and won, but the battle was executed when none needed to be. The only person pleased with winning is the one who initiated. Others walk away feeling defeated, while the battle initiator stands with his fist in the air. The battle is usually executed by one's ego. This card can reveal gossip, someone spreading lies, or a miscommunication and misunderstanding.

The Five of Swords is also about winning a battle where there were really are no benefits to it, except your ego felt that there was. It can also reveal someone who did something dodgy for personal gain. They obtained what they wanted through underhanded ways. Some in political power or in the corporate worlds could be accused of this and would receive this card to add indication.

In a love reading, this can show two people who are in a battle with one another. One or the both of you are experiencing excessive hurt or pride. It can be a date or lover taking advantage of you and you're unaware of it. Perhaps they're drawn to you because you always take care of things and pay the bill. The other partner becomes too comfortable with that and is not fully in love with you, but sticks around because they feel secure that you take care of things. This card would show up as a warning that they have an ulterior motive, even if they seem genuine on the surface.

If the Five of Swords is intended to describe someone, then it can say that this person is only out for themselves and doesn't care much about you, the relationship, or others. Thinking of oneself runs along that fine line, because to one extent it's not a bad thing that someone is focused on themselves pending it's not hurting anyone, but this would be a warning message if the person is with you for reasons of self-interest. This could also be the case in a work environment to describe someone as up to no good for personal gain. It can be that you're working in an environment with hostile people. Simple basic day-to-day conflict and challenges can bring this card up. You might be having a challenging day where it's one thing after another, then this card shows up to reveal that.

The Five of Swords in a reading can also point out that you may be having a battle or conflict with someone. The message here is to surrender as the fight isn't worth it even if you won. There are no winners in this particular ego based conflict. This can also point out a bully or an abuser around you, or you may be the bully without realizing it. The message here would warn you of this and to stop or there will be negative repercussions. You're ultimately not going to get your way even if you feel you won.

In a love relationship, it can show two people who are not seeing eye to eye or hearing one another. Usually in the traditional imagery of this card it shows someone holding several swords with a deceitful smirk of being satisfied as if they got away with murder. There are two swords on the ground with two people walking away hunched over as if defeated. This has many meanings in a read such as someone feeling as if they got away with something they intended to. It can be something criminal or dodgy. This can reveal you as the victim of such a person.

This isn't a pleasant card if it's a lover, since it can show the love partner was operating from ego in an argument with you instead of showing love and compassion. It can also be you who is the one that felt as if they won an unnecessary fight. This card points to someone who is being cocky or arrogant about it.

Another interpretation might be if it's a potential love interest and you're wondering why this person isn't contacting you, then this card could illustrate they have too much pride and ego. If you're not contacting them either, then you also have this same pride. One of you will need to fold and make the contact as the Five of Swords shows that both are refusing to for pride reasons. "Why should I make the move when he is the one that…" If that's the case, then neither will make a move. Someone will need to be the bigger person.

You've likely witnessed couples who seem to be constantly bickering, negative, or antagonistic, yet for some reason they insist on remaining in a relationship with one another. The Five of Swords would show such a fault finding connection. It's a stressful union to be in that points to a karmic tie that will need to be severed.

Six of Swords

The Six of Swords can indicate movement in a reading. It might be movement out of stormy waters and onto brighter pastures. This is one of the few less challenging Swords cards to get, but more welcoming. Because this can show movement, this card can also reveal travel even if it's a day trip.

Usually, the traditional image might show a figure sitting on a boat looking exhausted as if they had just been through an ordeal, but the boat ride is calm and soothing. This is the calm after the storm message as things start to relax after the hostile, defiant, and antagonistic Five of Swords card.

On a more challenging note, the Six of Swords can show you embarking on a journey where the destination is a big question mark or it is unclear. You are more or less winging it not knowing where it will lead. The Fool card can have a similar meaning, except with the Fool, the person is not concerned about where the road is going. They are happy go lucky regardless. The Six of Swords is mental and thinking related, so one would be concerned or apprehensive as the boat is floating away from one thing and hopefully towards something better. This is also the card of the seeker charting out new territories.

Six of Swords can have some measure of sadness or low feeling to it as you move along on a slow moving boat wrapped in a cloak slightly hunched over in weariness. One image description for the Six of Swords would be from the movie *Titanic* towards the end of the film where the character Rose has been rescued from the sinking ship and she's lost her new lover and family. She is wrapped in a blanket having no idea what awaits her from that point forward, but she has no choice but to continue on. Where will this boat take her now that her loved ones have died or have gone their own way? No one knows, but she has hope when she looks up and sees the Statue of Liberty as the boat sails past it and into America.

The Six of Swords shows someone who goes through each day moving along at work, but not particularly happy with where their life is. They just work through each day drudging along secretly longing for something passionate or spectacular to happen in their life. The message can indicate that you have the power to change things as the boat in the card is moving towards something.

The Six of Swords can point out what's to come with you months after a close loved one passes on or leaves you. You are left with the grief, but are soon coming out of it slightly changed and never quite the same again. You continue on your life path moving forward into new pastures as there is no other choice. This can be the card message of someone moving into recovery mode or beginning to feel happy and good about life again.

In a love reading, you might be single longing for a partner, then the Six of Swords can show you as being kind of down about it, but the plus about this is that you're sailing towards this partner so have no fear. This is especially the case if the following card is a positive love card.

In general, whether you will get that job, or you find a new love partner, the Six of Swords can show you moving gradually towards your goal or desire.

Seven of Swords

*T*he Seven of Swords in a reading can show someone being sneaky or cunning in some manner. This can include cheating in a love relationship or backhanded dealings at work. Someone is up to no good! It could be that a lover is chatting around with other people inappropriately or hiding something from you. While it might not be with the intention of meeting new prospects, this card is still warning that this person you're asking about doesn't seem to have any boundaries, therefore anything can happen beyond their control. There is reason for suspicion.

In the traditional typical image of the Seven of Swords, a figure can be seen escaping with the swords while dropping some of them in his path. This shows that someone is thinking they're getting away with a deceit, but they're being sloppy about it and could be caught or found out. They're not doing much to hide their actions.

My Spirit team has previously talked to me about the visible destruction of humanity in days like *Black Friday* in the United States. This is where you are able to witness greed as a dominant gene in some of human kind. The Seven of Swords would best describe that behavior. The media in general tends to be gossip oriented and manipulative rather than neutral and objective. This behavior would also be aligned with this card. Someone who will trample over others to obtain what they desire even though what they desire is not aligned with their higher self. The political arena or corporate areas tend to utilize underhanded methods to push themselves to the forefront. The Seven of Swords would also describe someone like that.

Sometimes this card can indicate that you're not facing an issue that you need to face head on. This might also be someone who is afraid of confrontation and will do anything to avoid having to face someone about an issue. Maybe this is someone who is afraid to talk to their superior at work about an issue. The Seven of Swords could be used to describe circumstances like this. It is not necessarily deceit that's at play every time you pull this card.

In a love relationship, the Seven of Swords can indicate deceit or cheating going on. This card may reveal that you want to leave your relationship, but are afraid to let your partner know. You may choose to avoid having to do the deed in some manner. This is by running away instead of dealing with it head on. Instead of telling your partner to their face, you may break up via text, email, social media, or by leaving a note on their door. The Seven of Swords could indicate this avoidance of confrontation or not wanting to face serious issues appropriately. Instead you choose to slink around it in a way that might seem inappropriate, dodgy, or cowardly.

The Seven of Swords may not always reveal something as detrimental as cheating or the ending of a relationship, but it can simply be that your partner has something on their mind that they're battling with that may or may not have anything to do with you. It doesn't involve cheating or leaving. It could be something that you'd be fine with hearing. Your partner has it in their mind that you might not want to hear it or they're afraid of your response.

This card can also show a partner who wants their independence and no longer wants to be in a love relationship. If the Three of Swords is next to it, then it could indeed be what's at play causing heartbreak in the process.

While single and dating, this card might show that you or this other potential have secrets that they're not saying and might be afraid to bring up. This card might also say that things won't work out as hoped or planned. It could be suggesting that you find another way or alternative, or to consider another possibility with something pertaining to the question asked. This card can also indicate someone who has trust issues with whoever they are involved with. The opposite is this card is telling you not to trust someone or something you're involved with.

The basic keywords of the Seven of Swords is stealing, lying, deceitfulness, secrets, being sneaky, avoiding, running away, escaping, betrayal, or lack of self-respect.

Eight of Swords

When the Eight of Swords shows up in a reading, it can be saying that you're not seeing things clearly. You're blinded by the truth or trapped and restricted from moving forward in some manner, but in the end the blocks erected are at your own hands. It's your mind that is giving the illusion of being trapped, when in truth you're free to do anything. This is the card of someone feeling victimized, acting like the victim, or putting themselves into a victim position desiring to be rescued in some way.

In the traditional imagery of the Eight of Swords, it shows someone blindfolded with rope wrapped around their body restricting their arms and hands from movement. Eight swords are in the ground surrounding the figure. You are able to take the blind fold off, remove the rope, and be freed to move forward, but you're feeling powerless as if this isn't the case. Generally, this is in your mind and has no basis of truth. Your own fears are putting up roadblocks that prevent you from making a move towards what you want.

The message of this card can be telling you to get out of your mind, avoid fear based thoughts, and don't listen to the voice of your dark ego. You can do anything you set your mind to. Don't allow fear to cripple you from moving forward. You're free to go in the direction of your dreams as this is what is intended for you.

This card can also be showing you to be living in isolation, but not for the reasons of personal spiritual growth and enlightenment, but rather in isolation due to fear. Perhaps you have social anxiety or are afraid to go outside. There is something that isn't connected to reality that is preventing you from coming out of isolation. The isolation isn't the welcoming kind of being alone where one needs to be with their thoughts or to recharge their batteries. The isolation in this card feels more like you're in prison. The Eight of Swords is self-imposed confinement. This card can also reveal you to be not thinking clearly. It is best to wait until clarity and calmness have entered the picture before making any rash decisions.

The Eight of Swords might pop up for someone who says, "Someone doesn't want me to move forward." With this card, it is a product of your own imagination. It is you that is restricting your own movement.

This can also show someone trapped in their current predicament at the hands of another. It might be a child or spouse who is living under the rule of an abusive or domineering and controlling person. Over time, the victim starts to feel powerless and trapped unable to make a move. In this case, the victim is not necessarily in that situation on their own accord especially if it's a child.

The Eight of Swords can also show someone who is bouncing from job to job not finding something they enjoy doing to stick with. You might feel directionless or as if you are floundering all over the place. This card would also show up for someone who refuses to go after their dreams. They will make pessimistic excuses such as, "They won't hire me. I'm not pretty enough." It'll be one excuse after another from the Eight of Swords person. The justifications one makes are the darkness of ego convincing you that you're not worthy or deserving of what you want. Everyone is worthy enough to go after what they desire.

In a love reading, if you're single this can be saying that your fears are preventing a lover from coming in. Perhaps there is something restricting you from obtaining a lover. The lover may be around you in the vicinity, but you're not noticing them. They could have been presented to you, but something is preventing you from seeing them.

If you have your eye on someone romantically, and you pull this card as to what their feelings are, then this might be saying they have fears or worries about approaching you or getting into a relationship. There is something blocking them from making a move. Surrounding cards can indicate an outcome or overall general consensus.

There may be positive love cards with the Eight of Swords, then this could indicate someone is attracted to you, but worried or hesitant to making any kind of move. They might have low self-esteem or feel unworthy to be with someone like you. If you pulled the card for you about this other person, then it could be you who has the low self-esteem, or feeling like you can't measure up to them and that you don't stand a chance. The Eight of Swords shows that it is you putting up these false restrictions.

If this is about a current love relationship, it can say that you or your partner are feeling trapped in the connection, or one of you is afraid to approach the other one about an issue. This doesn't necessarily indicate a break up, but if someone is feeling trapped or stifled in a connection, then something will need to change in the relationship in order to eliminate suffocation, or someone will leave.

In the end, the general meaning of the Eight of Swords is someone who feels restricted from movement, trapped by their circumstances, or blocked from making a move. The Eight of Swords ultimately says that you have the power to get out of your circumstance, so find ways that release the bonds and self-imprisonment in order to begin moving forward.

Nine of Swords

The Nine of Swords in a reading points to despair, depression, insomnia, and anxiety based feelings. The anguish that's experienced is typically in your mind and not based in truth. It can be that you're experiencing endless anxiety over any issue in your life, but this card is indicating that it's mostly your mind creating unnecessary drama out of nothing.

This can also be a card that shows someone having nightmares in a dream state, or they're battling with bad insomnia unable to be awake or fall asleep.

The traditional image of the card shows someone sitting up in bed with their face in their hand in despair. Nine swords are lined up on top of each other on the wall behind them illustrating a prison like feeling. The shot is intended to take place at night because it's no surprise that one's worries and anxiety climb in the middle of the night. The reason is you're lying there left with nothing to do, but entertain all of those random thoughts. You're not busy partaking in activities during the day that keep your mind distracted from the disparity of your situation or circumstance your anxiety is about.

At night, the darkness contributes to even more sadness since there is nothing bright and happy about the dark. Some people have stated when having trouble with a lover or a friend that when they receive an email or text from them late at night just before bed that they don't want to read it until the next morning. This is because they fear reading something that might upset them preventing them from sleeping. The Nine of Swords can indicate this feeling in you.

If this is a work related reading, the Nine of Swords can reveal worry connected to a job or career. Maybe you had an interview and are unsure of how it went, but you really want this job. You're kept up all night thinking about it unable to break the constant low vibrational thoughts.

In a love reading, the Nine of Swords can show you to be having fears or anxiety surrounding a relationship or the lack of a relationship. If you're in a relationship, then the fears might be that your partner is up to no good, even though there is no concrete evidence or proof of this. You might have seen something that could be questionable. Perhaps you heard a statement made by your partner that has your mind thinking and going crazy that there is something up. Typically, this card points to it all being in your mind. Surrounding cards can offer more clarity, since the Nine of Swords is not a card that is known for its clarity. The person is usually too absorbed in their mind to be seeing or thinking clearly.

This card can show up whenever there is any anxiety based emotions going on that also keep you up all night lying in bed staring at the ceiling thinking worry filled thoughts. It can be that you met a new love potential for the first time. The meeting date might have gone well, but later when you don't hear from the other person your mind starts spinning. You start to kick yourself wondering if you blew it or said something wrong. You start obsessing, "I'm sure I was being weird and made a complete fool of myself. They must've been sorely disappointed with who I turned out to be and I blew this one." You're up all night thinking about it because you like this person, but don't know what else to do.

The Nine of Swords is a Minor Arcana card and can blow in and out in a matter of days pending you speed things along to resolve whatever it is that is causing you upset. Days later you end up hearing from the potential mate that they enjoyed you and would like to see you again. Suddenly the Nine of Swords energy evaporates and you're on cloud nine again. This could especially be the case if you have positive love cards sitting alongside the Nine of Swords.

While the Nine of Swords is not the most pleasant card to get, sometimes it serves as a warning that if you're in your mind unable to escape the trappings within it that you will want to work on calming your thoughts and getting out of your head. Come to the reality that much of the anxiety and fears in your mind are conjured up by the darkness of your ego. It's not always based in truth. If something happened to cause you anxiety, then work on getting over it. There's nothing that can be done. Any embarrassment you felt about a situation you were in is usually not as bad as you're making it out to be.

If one wanted to find out the outcome of a love relationship or a job or anything at all and you receive the Nine of Swords card in the last future position, then it could indicate that the circumstance will be bathed in anxiety. The anxiety could also be mostly in your mind. Don't give other people that kind of power over you.

The Nine of Swords could serve as a warning that perhaps your fears about a situation are true. The Tarot is so complex and tricky that you could get a double meaning with the Nine of Swords. One of them being that the fears you feel about a situation could be true or the fears are all in your head. Surrounding cards can indicate more information, or trust your instincts and divine guidance as to what it is. If you're feeling something strongly, then it could likely be true or the energy of what you're feeling is true. Sudden dark feelings are not the Devil, they are the ego, which is the real Devil in humankind.

In the end, the Nine of Swords can show someone who is suffering in some manner that is typically brought on by the fears and the ego part of their consciousness. You can break away from this if you work on exercises to keep your mind positive and away from self-fulfilling prophecies. Usually what's created in the mind is something being made out to be worse than it actually is.

Ten of Swords

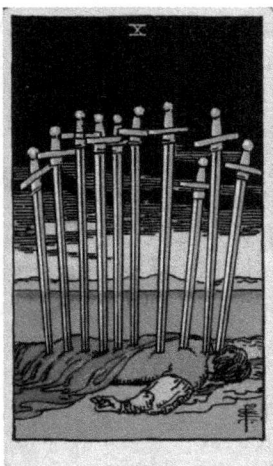

The Ten of Swords card in a reading tends to be one of the scarier looking cards in the Swords suit next to the Three of Swords. The Ten of Swords usually shows a human figure with ten swords stabbed into their lifeless body on the ground. The overall tone of the card is dark and foreboding as if a death has taken place. The Ten of Swords is not always as negative or as challenging as the image depicts. The visual is a metaphor of something that has ended, but when something ends, this paves the way for something better. Usually the Ten of Swords can indicate the end of one way of thinking or the death of your former self in order to be reborn again.

The Ten of Swords is the end of one chapter within one lifetime. Perhaps a relationship or job has ended, or the way you view circumstances has ended. This follows the Nine of Swords, which was a card that showed anxiety ridden thoughts about a situation wondering if something is true or not. The Ten of Swords is one step above that where you discovered the anxiety ridden thoughts you had about a situation were true. Maybe it was that your partner was indeed betraying you. It can feel like the end of the world, but the Ten of Swords is as low as you can get. What follows is a brand new beginning. You slam the door shut on one chapter and open it to reveal a brighter one.

The Ten of Swords shows the truth coming to light leaving you in a deathly like state. This is the end of that cycle, because once you move through the feelings of accepting this new change and truth, you are able to rebuild yourself stronger opening up the door to something even better than what you previously had. It might not be seen or believed while you're going through the turmoil, but the Ten of Swords usually shows the end of the worst. Now you know the truth and can proceed forward down the more appropriate path.

The Ten of Swords signifies death, but a metaphorical death, and the ending of one situation. It is much like the Death card in the Major Arcana, except the Death card is an ending that takes a much longer time to transform, whereas the Ten of Swords can be a much quicker transformation that can happen within weeks, rather than months if it were the Death card that popped up.

If you received the Ten of Swords in terms of the outcome of a situation, then this can serve as a warning that it might not end well. In this case, you can alter your path and go down an entirely different road that keeps you away from the inevitable forecast of the Ten of Swords. If it's a job you should take or a potential relationship partner you should go after, the Ten of Swords can be warning you against it. It can say that if you go after it, then it might not be what you hoped it would be.

On a metaphysical level, the Ten of Swords can show psychological breakdown, disaster, failure, or simple mental exhaustion. Blessings arise out of challenges you currently face.

On a literal level, the card can be warning of someone trying to sabotage you, bad mouthing, gossip, or stabbing you in the back. The Ten of Swords can reveal that the worst is yet to come or the worst has already happened. If you have positive cards following the Ten of Swords in a spread, then it can show that you've already experienced the worst, and it's nothing but smoothing sailing moving forward. In this case, then the Ten of Swords would be a welcome relief.

It can sometimes be confusing distinguishing the meaning between the Nine of Swords and the Ten of Swords. The Nine of Swords is anxiety ridden emotions that are fear based or ego based and not necessarily proven to be of truth. The Ten of Swords anxiety is finding out the truth of a situation where it's crystal clear that it's over or concluded and true. The positive side to this is that you've already hit rock bottom and there's no more room in the bottomless pit to fall. Like the Shania Twain song "Up", you can only go up from here and circumstances will be improving.

Page of Swords

PAGE of SWORDS.

PERSON:

The Page of Swords can reveal a young person under 25 who has an Air sign in the top tier of their chart. This is Aquarius, Gemini, Libra. *(Top tier can be Sun sign, Rising, Moon, Venus, Mars)*

If they do not have those stats, then this is someone regardless of age or sign who is an original thinker who loves to dissect and analyze. They are a wordy communicative genius in many respects having a larger vocabulary than those similar to their age. They govern their life through logic and ideas rather than emotion. This is someone who appears rather serious or as if they're angry about something, yet they are perfectly happy. Their expressions can give others mixed signals as to how they're feeling. This is because they perceive things from a different space than those around them.

This can be a super chatty person peppering someone with constant inquisitive questions. Like all of the Pages, there is some measure of naivety present. They can be prone to gossip or being secretive and dodgy. At the same time, they're structured and follow the rules. They speak up when they see an injustice or bullying of any kind happening. Yet, they might also be the bully with their words not realizing it. This can be the young talkative student who is always visiting their teacher to have intellectual banter. They crave knowledge and mental stimulation.

MESSENGER:

Will the person contact me? This is the least romantic of all the Pages, but any contact is better than no contact. The Page of Swords can show someone contacting you via text, email, or phone call, but it's not a romantic reach out. It's usually just a, "Hi, how are you?" The Page of Swords message is distant, impersonal, and cold, but some would rather have that kind of reach out than having no reach out at all. For the Page of Swords, this is about all they can muster when reaching out, which can still show some measure of interest.

The Page of Swords in a reading can show that an important message may be delivered to you in a harsh, blunt, or tactless way. Don't shoot the messenger, but instead look at the message being relayed. The message has truth to it or involves an answer about something you need to know.

SITUATION:

The Page of Swords in a reading is no different than many of the Swords cards, and that means there can be some tumultuous energy surrounding it. Typically, in the Tarot many of the Page of Swords images show some dark clouds hovering over the figure to symbolize this. It can be that circumstances may not go exactly as expected.

This can be about someone who is interested in relationships where they can learn something. They prefer older, wiser, or more experienced partners as they feel intellectually stimulated and challenged. This might normally shy away others, but not the Page of Swords who is starving for mental stimulation and friendship camaraderie. This is regardless of their age and sign.

The Page of Swords message is about the truth regardless if it's good or bad. They uphold justice and truth in their dealings with others. If they feel stifled or suffocated in any manner, then they may be cutting or snappy with their words in retaliation and will ultimately leave.

This message is also about taking the bull by the horns and being the initiator whether you want to or not. The Page of Swords can be the start of an intellectual relationship. This is one that starts off with chatting first for a long while before it moves into more. Even when it moves into more, it still feels like a friendship or companionship more than anything else.

Knight of Swords

KNIGHT of SWORDS .

PERSON:

The Knight of Swords can reveal someone around 25-35 who has an Air sign in the top tier of their chart. This is Aquarius, Gemini, Libra. *(Top tier can be Sun sign, Rising, Moon, Venus, Mars)*

If they do not have those stats, then this is someone regardless of age or sign who is quick in their thinking. They waste no time cutting to the truth of the matter. This Knight challenges others and governs their life through logic rather than heart. They may be cutting and blunt, but they have no time or interest in tip toeing around feelings. Their mind moves too swiftly to stop and smell the roses with delicate fingers. This person respects themselves before anyone else. They don't respect authority or other people's rules. They've got a sharp mind and need to use it on noble causes or they'll keep moving. This person can be rebellious and ruthless.

In relationships, the Knight of Swords requires intellectual stimulation first before falling in love. If the mental connection is not there, then they won't have much interest. They need to be challenged intellectually and love debating as it excites them. They need someone who can match that or doesn't shy away from it. They like independent minded free thinking people who don't follow the crowd and who are a bit unusual in some way.

SITUATION:

The Knight of Swords in a reading says to use your mind and think logically in a situation. If you've been over emotional about something, then this message can be saying to reserve emotion in this circumstance in order to receive clarity.

This also says if you've got great ideas wondering if you should move forward with them, then this Knight says yes, charge on in without hesitation. This can also show issues surrounding someone disrespecting you or you dissing them. It can be that someone is trying to stir up conflict with you or you with them.

The Knight of Swords can also be asking you to research new ideas and work on developing them. This would also be including taking a class or seminar around the area of your interest to gain wisdom and strengthen your intellect.

This Knight also indicates quick swift changes and movement. These changes can be challenging or blessings depending on surrounding cards or the question being asked.

In relationships, a potential can be all talk and no action, or this is the basis of the relationship in general.

The Knight of Swords can also be to stand up for yourself, speak your mind, and say what you want.

Queen of Swords

QUEEN of SWORDS.

PERSON:

The Queen of Swords can reveal someone around aged 35 and above who has an Air sign in the top tier of their chart. This is Aquarius, Gemini, Libra. *(Top tier can be Sun sign, Rising, Moon, Venus, Mars)*

If they do not have those stats, then this is someone regardless of age or sign who always believes they are right. Most of the time they are, but they can be incredibly tactless on occasion that it can rub some people the wrong way. There is little emotion or compassion in their mannerisms and communication. This is someone who is all about ideas, thinking, communication, and logic. This is also a wise soul who knows it all. They are a teacher and thinker. When this person executes instructions, they expect others to follow it, and get it right the first time. If not, then you're banished as they have high ideals and expectations.

This person can cut others with their words. You don't want to get on their bad side or into a debate with them, because they usually always win. This person makes a great advocate and fighter for the underdog. They have humanitarian gifts and are self-reliant. They are also impatient and expect things to happen immediately without delay.

The Queen of Swords has great humor, so even though this person may deliver tactless information or statements, they can often bring lighthearted humor to it that softens the blow too.

SITUATION:

The Queen of Swords in a reading can be asking you to express what you're thinking and feeling to others if you haven't been. It can be to gain wisdom and knowledge around a circumstance. This is also about getting to the heart of the matter and find the truth. Eliminate anything or anyone that is not beneficial to your growth.

The Queen of Swords is the Queen that cuts others out. This message can indicate a separation whether it's a friendship or lover. This is not the happiest or most positive card necessarily to get in a love relationship reading. Because it can show divorce, a separation, or split. If this is the case, understand that break ups happen for a reason. There can be someone else that will be entering the picture. The person you're currently with hasn't been good for you. This might also show someone who is commitment phobic or not looking for a committed relationship.

In a love reading, the Queen of Swords shows someone who is super independent while in a relationship. While all of the Queens are independent, the Queen of Swords is independent to the point where this person doesn't need to be in a relationship. It's not what drives this person. While in the relationship, this person may be off doing their own thing. An understanding partner who allows this kind of freedom would work for this person. They don't jive with co-dependent or emotional needy people, and could end up leaving if that is the case.

The Queen of Swords asks you to be up front, direct, and honest. Don't worry about feelings, but speak your truth. This message can also show that the truth will be revealed if you're needing an answer to something. The truth may or may not be what you want to hear, but the blessings in this will be that you will no longer be in the dark. In the end, this is about being quick in your thinking and make a decision without wasting any time.

King of Swords

KING of SWORDS.

PERSON:

The King of Swords can reveal someone around aged 35 and above who has an Air sign in the top tier of their chart. This is Aquarius, Gemini, Libra. *(Top tier can be Sun sign, Rising, Moon, Venus, Mars)*

If they do not have those stats, then this is someone regardless of age or sign who is completely in control, a great strategist, and conversationalist. They are an original thinker who rules with words and thoughts. Their general disposition tends to be on the harsher cold side. This is because they don't usually use tact when they communicate. They are direct and to the point and have no time to be politically correct. They say what they mean and mean what they say. You know exactly where you stand with them.

This person might be a lawyer or work in the political or legal sphere on some level such as a judge or politician, or they can be a police officer, or in the military. They would make a great judge because they don't use emotion when making decisions. They hear all of the facts and have crystal clear objective insight. They would not be found on the comment boards on media, news, or gossip sites because they have a higher view of situations than the general public is unable to reach. They are fair and don't allow their emotions or ego to get away with them. This is also someone who is Claircognizant having the gift of clear knowing.

The King of Swords is a know it all, and most of the time they do indeed know it all! This is a quick thinker and someone who can see the entire picture laid out before them. They have no time or interest in emotional demands or scenes. Anyone that gets in his way of his goals are immediately cut out without so much as a word or thought. Stand with him and you have a devoted loyal friend for life.

Typically, those in the air element may be difficult to know or understand as far as what their interest level is, because they come from a logical space where they always look as if they're deep in serious thought no matter what the occasion is.

For someone who might have a romantic interest in them, this can cause initial confusion as to how deep their interest might be in return. It's also easy to fall for them because they are talkative, sociable, and attentive. This doesn't mean they are romantically interested. If they are romantically interested, they can suddenly change on a whim if they feel someone they're with is either not standing by them or making emotional demands. They'll cut that person right out without a thought. They rule by thoughts and not emotions. Therefore, their interest can shift as quickly as the wind. They make better friends than lovers, but fear not as they tend to fall for those who keep them mentally stimulated and curious. The more unusual someone is the better as it keeps them guessing while preventing boredom from sinking in. In a relationship, he is usually distant and remote. He looks at the partnership like any other business partnership, but is capable of going the distance.

SITUATION:

The King of Swords in a general situation reading can be asking you to use less emotion and more logic in a particular situation. Observe circumstances from an analytical viewpoint. This can be to also cut out what no longer serves you. Do it without reservation or emotion. Take the knowledge you've gained and put it into action. If you're stuck on making a decision, then the King of Swords says to use fairness and balance when coming to the conclusion. Look at all sides and choices and then honor that accordingly.

On another note, if you've been cut off emotionally, are generally a cold person, or you have been aloof, then the King of Swords is asking you to do the opposite. Bring in some feeling and emotion to a situation and don't be so distant.

In love, this may show that you have interest in someone whose feelings haven't been revealed. You're in a state of confusion not knowing how they feel about you. If you're in a relationship, then it might show a partner consumed with work or who is not highly romantic and sentimental. If you're looking for someone to sweep you off your feet, get passionate with you, or shower you with gifts and attention, then you'll be barking up the wrong tree with the King of Swords.

The King of Swords can indicate a great friendship that turns into a committed relationship through mutual interests, values, causes, and communication style. It may be lacking in passion, but it makes up for it in a best friendship with this person.

Pentacles/Earth

The suit of Pentacles focuses on areas surrounding material comforts, security, home, career, and finances. It resides in the element of Earth which is the more grounding of all the elements. Astrologically it represents the signs of Taurus, Virgo, and Capricorn. The Pentacles can sometimes be called Coins or Discs in some Tarot decks ruling the physical and material world. Since Earthly life is primarily concerned with possessions, this suit is especially loved due to what it can reveal surrounding physical concrete material circumstances in one's life including career, home life, and finances.

Ace of Pentacles

*T*he Ace of Pentacles in a reading can show positive growth or gradual movement upwards in the realms of abundance or blessings surrounding the question asked. Aces are beginnings of whatever the suit energy is. The Ace of Pentacles can indicate new positive beginnings surrounding a money making venture or stronger stability. This can include a new job or more prosperity flowing to you.

The Ace of Pentacles can be movement in the career arena, with relationships, or with your body through physical activity. The Ace of Pentacles can give one a feeling of being satisfied or a stronger sense of well-being.

The typical image of the Ace of Pentacles is a hand in the air holding a huge coin. This is relaying that happiness lies in your hand. You have the power to manifest what you desire. It can be the one seed you're about to plant or have planted which will soon begin to show some return. It's the start of a great plan that can bring in positive rewards. It can indicate new contracts being signed whether it's a business deal, house, bank, credit card, or investment accounts. This can also be inheritance, lottery, or gambling winnings.

In a love reading, the Ace of Pentacles can show the potential for a stable and secure relationship that can go the distance. If one is deep in a relationship, then this card can be indicating that this is a solid connection of mutual appreciation. Expect a period of deepening and bonding more than usual. It shows stability on the horizon with the current direction it's headed down.

If one is wondering what a potential sees in them, then this card can be saying that they view you as stable. Those looking to get into a long term relationship are turned on by stability and a partner who is together and grounded, so this would be a positive trait to have. On a shallow level, this potential might see you as someone who would help them out financially. They know they would be secure with you in that respect. It's one of the factors about you that appeals to them. This doesn't necessarily equate to them taking advantage of you unless you allow that.

If you were recently seeing someone, the Ace of Pentacles can show that the relationship has a strong foundation from which to start. All the positives are in place, but it does not mean it will go the distance. It says that the relationship has the potential to last as long as both parties do something about it, which they are both capable of. This is a pairing of emotional stable and secure partners who appreciate longevity.

If you're looking to find out how you're going to meet a potential, then the Ace of Pentacles may indicate through some kind of work related endeavor. It can be connected to a colleague, or you bump into this person during work hours outside on a break. You come across one another through some connection with work.

In the end, the Ace of Pentacles can show positive abundance surrounding anything pertaining to physical or material longings. This can be through work, career, investments, inheritance, or financial flow and movement. Because it is an Ace, it is the beginnings of that. You're basically off to a great start. Ace of Pentacles also represents body, mind, spirit exercises, as well as the need to ground yourself, or that you have positive physical health.

Two of Pentacles

*T*he Two of Pentacles can show someone juggling too many things at once. This card asks you to ensure you're balancing everything out enough so that you don't experience burn out. This means balancing work and home life. It can also show that you're in the middle of change, or you're required to be flexible about an issue. This can also indicate someone who has two jobs. One might be a job that pays the bills, while the other is a life purpose hobby that isn't bringing in enough financially to quit the day job.

Juggling and balance are the keywords associated with the Two of Pentacles. The traditional image tends to show someone trying to balance two pentacles or coins with one leg up. The coins form the 8 symbol of infinity and abundance. Behind him are two ships riding on stormy seas.

Ultimately, the Two of Pentacles is neither positive nor negative, but neutral. It is a reminder to ensure you're keeping everything balanced. At the same time, this card can show someone who knows how to balance quite a bit. They are a brilliant multi-tasker and can handle life's challenges as swiftly as a Fireman answering a bell. The person in the image of this card doesn't appear to be stressed or unhappy. He's busy chugging along and handling whatever is thrown at him with ease.

The Two of Pentacles also points to someone having fun and enjoying life. It is advising you to slow down and have some fun as you're juggling too many responsibilities. Since the Pentacles tends to deal with work and money concerns, this can be showing someone who has money that comes in and out or slips through their fingers. Money comes in from unexpected sources and flies out just as quickly. They are always on a budget, but seem to have enough of a cushion to survive. This isn't without its stresses as they may wonder when the next pay check is coming in at certain times.

In a love reading, this can show someone who is dating around or juggling two or more dates. You can be asking about a potential and if there is a possibility for you two, then this could indicate that the other person, or the both of you seem to have quite a bit going on in your lives. It doesn't mean they're not interested, but this is someone who is going through a phase of juggling too much at once with no time for a love partner, even if they want one. In a love relationship, this can show a partner who is currently distracted with other day-to-day practicalities outside of love. The couple is busy with working and will need to inject some personal fun couple time.

You're wondering why the person you have your eye on doesn't text or call, the Two of Pentacles can show them as being busy and having too many distractions around them or too much going on in their life. It is typically work that is the distraction, but not always.

If you're single, this card might say that you have two choices for love prospects and you will need to make a decision on which one you have more interest in. This can also be said about two job prospects. It can show a creative person juggling two projects at the same time. This may even show someone dating a couple of people at the same time trying to keep it all balanced.

What are some personality traits of this incoming potential? Two of Pentacles suggests they might have two jobs, or be exceptional at business, prioritizing, and time management in their life. They seem to be busy able to fill every minute with something.

Three of Pentacles

*T*he Three of Pentacles can show you joining with one or more people becoming a stronger team. When you have two separate strong people join together, then that multiplies making magic happen. This is regardless if it is career, friendship, or love. This is working together as a team.

This can also show the completion of a project and sharing it with others. If you've been working on building your business or working to get positively noticed at your job, then this is a good sign that you're heading in the right direction. Keep doing what you're doing even if you're not seeing results yet, as this tends to indicate the results are forthcoming as long as you continue on.

Usually the Three of Pentacles shows someone who is good at what they do, even if they are new at their trade or job. They are someone who will dive on into something and excel at it. This shows financial rewards for your work efforts. It can indicate some kind of job promotion or a raise. It can be that someone of importance notices the work you do and offers praise or compensation. If you're asking about finances, then this is also a positive one to get indicating improvement in that arena.

If you're wondering how you're going to do at a new job or with a new project, then this can show that you'll master it and do exceptionally well. It may suggest some form of notoriety or extra compensation as a result. It will definitely look good on your resume and work credentials as you continue to build towards your dreams. If you're interested in pursuing a trade, career, or relationship, then this can be asking you to plan and strategize how you are going to do that.

The Ace of Pentacles might have been the beginnings of a new project or job, while the Two of Pentacles was showing the juggling of work and trying to maintain balance as you get into the groove of your job, while the Three of Pentacles shows the beginnings of positive return coming in. It shows signs of excelling at what you do. This is someone who works hard for the money without having things handed to them. If you've been working hard and seeing no results, then this is a welcome relief that it's coming so keep the faith.

In a love relationship, if you're wondering if someone has any interest in you, then the Three of Pentacles says yes. While this might not be the most romantic hearts and flowers kind of card, it does show practical longevity. This potential sees you as someone who they would love to team up with romantically. They have their head about themselves and feel as if you two would be better together than solo. This would reveal a strong couple who works as a team.

The Three of Pentacles may also show a third party introducing you to a potential. If you're in a relationship it can be asking the couple to compromise on a circumstance, or work together rather than opposing one another. This can be about making plans to become more committed, which can include moving into together. This card is more or less the planning stages of your next move. It can also mean that the couple has been working in harmony more than they ever have. This includes contributing on things together whether it's splitting the bill or rent. This is a couple who are the true definition of equal partners.

Will you ever meet the next lover? The Three of Pentacles says yes. Start making plans to ready yourself for this person even if it means changing certain toxic habits and cleaning up your act.

Four of Pentacles

*T*he Four of Pentacles can show you to be hoarding your possessions never parting with them. This is especially the case if you have money. There are people with money who might not have been born into money, but had to work hard for it. When they have obtained enough riches to last their lifetime, they still function as if they're poor. The Four of Pentacles can show this imbalance of energy where they are holding the finances too tightly out of fear. The flip side is they are spending too frivolously and need to slow down or use caution. This could be that you're afraid of risks and overly cautious with a life decision.

In terms of work, this can indicate that a company or employee could be strict, by the book, and structure oriented to the point that it stifles imaginative creativity. Creativity is about thinking outside the box and going against the norm. It gets the energy flowing, which in turn gets abundance flowing. This might also suggest a bad investment or a financial loss. The opposite end of the spectrum is an investment would need to be made.

In a love relationship, if you're curious about why your flirtatious advances are not being returned, then this might show the person to being overly cautious when it comes to love and afraid to take that leap. Someone could be into you, but is hesitant to making a move. This can also be someone who is stubborn and resistant to change. The Four of Pentacles can show someone who is reserved or withdrawn. They're holding back over fear of lack.

While dating or in a relationship with someone, then the Four of Pentacles might imply it is either of you as being super possessive with a need to dominate. It can also indicate that one of you is hanging onto the other one for dear life out of fear of losing the other person.

The Four of Pentacles might show someone who is inflexible, resistant to change, overly cautious, or even greedy. It is the card that can point to someone going from one extreme to another, whether that is in belief systems, values, or desires. They might fear loss of what they've gained or made, whether it's a love relationship, or fear of losing a job, or income. The Four of Pentacles could represent the Scrooge character from *The Christmas Carol*. A man who has made endless money, but he's afraid to part with even a tiny amount of it. This also shows someone who is afraid of making any moves in life for fear of losing.

In love, the Four of Pentacles doesn't necessarily mean someone isn't interested, but they are holding back for ego reasons whether it's fear of rejection or fear of being in a relationship. You might be wondering if a current relationship will ever be more committed. This card shows that the person may have interest, but is afraid to take that leap. The Four of Pentacles can also indicate someone holding back or withholding affection out of punishment. This would be the case if you did something to bruise their ego. People hold grudges in all connections when there is a fight. This card can show someone giving the silent treatment or having a chip on their shoulder. The personality traits of a potential here can show someone who might be guarded and difficult to penetrate. If surrounding cards show more open and affectionate love relationship cards, then this can show that the person will open up over time and end up bringing incredible love into the connection. Some who start off guarded or shy expect the other person to work for their affections. They don't automatically give it on a whim to just anyone.

Five of Pentacles

The Five of Pentacles can indicate a loss of some kind. Because it's in the Earth suit, the loss can be a financial or security based one, or it shows that you're struggling to make ends meet.

The Five of Pentacles can also indicate poor or struggling health, illness, or feeling run down and exhausted regularly. It can also show someone who feels isolated and disconnected from everyone. They sometimes feel as if the whole world is against them.

In a general reading, this can be warning you to budget for the time being as there could be some financial loss that comes out of nowhere. This can also point to a bad purchase regardless if you have money or not. This is where you're more or less throwing money away over something that doesn't work out. This could also indicate a job loss.

The Five of Pentacles can suggest that it is time to budget and keep a steady eye out on what's happening around you so there are no losses. This can show someone who lives paycheck to paycheck, which is pretty much most of the working class and world. But if it's showing up in a reading and that's what it's about, then it can mean that it affects you more than others who just accept it without thinking much of it.

The Five of Pentacles can also show someone who is unhappy with the kind of work they do. It might be a dull job that pays the bills, but it's not fulfilling on a passionate level. It's not your life purpose work.

In a love reading, the Five of Pentacles can suggest that a partner is feeling abandoned by a lover, even if they are in a loving relationship. They might be going through a period where they are feeling lonely and their partner is busy with other things and not reaching out. This can cause strife and strain if the other partner doesn't offer some measure of support.

Many partake in posting on social media. When someone is feeling unloved in general, they might post something on social media to illicit a positive response or praise from friends and followers. The Five of Pentacles might show up for someone in a reading at that time when it is being done in heavy abundance. You're going through a period of needing to be propped up by others.

This card can also be how one feels after a break up, which is abandoned. It shows someone struggling to move on, even though they are moving on without choice.

If you're single and asking how it will go if you approach someone, then this card can show that you may be rejected. While that can be a total blow to receive this card about someone you like, then you can always give it a shot and see how it goes. If you do end up being rejected, at least you had this card to armor yourself before approaching the person. When you did approach them, then you did so knowing that it might not go well. The blow is less harsh when you walk in knowing it's the way it can go.

The Tarot is helpful, but in the end follow your internal guide. If you feel strongly about someone, then ask them out regardless that you received this card. The worst that can happen is they say no. The rejection in this card can be a temporary one. It might just be the wrong time to approach someone. They reject you, but later they come around to say they are interested.

The Five of Pentacles might also show that the person you're interested in doesn't have much to offer in a relationship or is not looking to get into one.

A single person might receive this card if their self-esteem has plummeted from not having a lover. They feel that it has something to do with them and that no one wants them or loves them.

In the traditional Tarot image of this card, it shows two figures moving through the cold snow hunched over wearing tattered run down rags. They are of low means, struggling, and have experienced hard times. They're walking past a church with a stain glass window, which shows there is hope if they look around to notice it.

The overall essence of the Five of Pentacles is someone experiencing tough times in their life. They are feeling abandoned, rejected, or excluded. They've experienced feelings of being denied or had a loss of some kind. This can even be a temporary loss of faith or hope. It can be criticism or a statement darted your way that brought you down. Look to other cards in the spread for glimmers of how the situation will transform, or use this to increase your hope and faith surrounding a circumstance.

Six of Pentacles

*T*he Six of Pentacles in a reading shows an influx in income. It can reveal sudden additional monies coming in. It can be through a job raise, inheritance, lotteries, gambling's, etc. The typical image of the Six of Pentacles shows two people kneeling down before a well-dressed standing figure who drops money in their hands. This card can indicate that it is you who is receiving abundance, or that you are the figure standing who is helping someone else out. It would be asking you to give of your time, assistance, or money to someone who needs your help.

Abundance with this card is not necessarily financial. It can be positive abundance in other ways such as giving to someone through a kind gesture or helpful therapeutic words. It can show you as being the recipient of someone else's compassion. The message here can also be asking you to request help from another party. This other person offers assistance surrounding your question. The Six of Pentacles says that help is forthcoming in unexpected ways.

In some cards, the Six of Pentacles reveals a scale with a hand dropping coins into the tray of one of the scales. This is to indicate balancing out your finances or your life in general. This can also be showing circumstances improving and positively flowing into your life.

When you reach a certain high position, then the message is asking you to share the abundance. This doesn't necessarily mean financially, but this can indicate donating to charities. This can be about someone who has money and doesn't need to work if they don't want to, but the card message is asking you to find other ways to be productive. Find a hobby or passion you enjoy that can benefit others. This would fit the Six of Pentacles guidance of giving to those in need. The message can also be showing that you're already doing that or that you are giving too much away and need to reign it in to keep it balanced. This can also be a positive message that shows an approval of a loan or a job raise.

In a love reading, you're asking about the personality of someone, then the Six of Pentacles can show that they are a giving person, charitable, or a humanitarian. They do well financially and have a cushion to breath and not worry about paying their bills.

In a relationship, the message can be donating more of your time to your partner. Perhaps you've been consumed and perpetually busy with work that you've been neglecting your love partner. You need to incorporate balance in giving to your partner in some way. This message can also reveal a couple who has a constant flow of giving and receiving going on between one another. They are a happy balanced couple who make the relationship work together.

This card might also show a Teacher/Student type relationship, where one of the partners is a mentor to the other. The Six of Pentacles may also show an age difference of seven to ten years or more between the partners.

This message can indicate where you could meet a potential love partner. Perhaps it's somewhere that is affiliated with a charity, or they find you through a work related endeavor. You'll have mutual interests and exchanges moving back and forth.

The Six of Pentacles can also show a couple who is not balanced. Perhaps one of the partners is too co-dependent that it is causing friction with the other one. If emotions are not on the same level between partners, then this creates imbalance.

This is a card of giving or receiving. If you're financially well to do, then it could be to donate to charities or those less fortunate. If you're struggling in any form, then this could be a sign of abundance to come. This could be in the form of money, a new job/career, or a good deed done for you.

Giving and receiving keeps the energy flow balanced in your life. This isn't always financial flow. It can be the giving of one's time to help someone else. This is a positive card, but also a reminder for those that have too much, to give some of your time or money to help the less fortunate.

The Six of Pentacles can reveal you to be a mentor passing on wisdom to a student type, or that you are the recipient of this wisdom from another.

If you've been working on a project and wondering about its success, then this also points to it being successful with positive returns. If you've been on a spiritual path, then expect it to move to the next plateau.

With love, this could be added support from a love interest, or that your current relationship becomes more balanced and on an even keel. If you're single, you may meet someone who is your equal.

Seven of Pentacles

$\mathcal{T}$he Seven of Pentacles is a great card to receive for those waiting for something to happen pertaining to their question. The message of this card is saying that what you want is coming, but just not yet. The not yet part is what can cause frustration. Some have protested to not like this card when they see it in a spread because it doesn't seem to shout an instant yes. However, a *not yet* is better than a definite no. This is saying that what you desire is coming, so have patience and keep doing what you're doing. It may feel as if you're playing the waiting game, but this is a positive sign that results are on the way. There may be delays or roadblocks beyond your control. Patience, trust, and faith are needed at this time.

This indicates slow moving progress surrounding whatever you're asking. It's not saying that it won't happen, but that it will gradually. The Seven of Pentacles shows a farmer or gardener has been busy outside planting seeds. He's watching the seeds blossom into crops, flowers, trees, etc. He stands patiently as if waiting for more to happen. This is someone who is putting in an effort into something, but not seeing much return in this diligence. The Seven of Pentacles asks you to have patience as the results may be delayed, but they are forthcoming.

This is also an indication to stop and give yourself a pat on the back for how much work you've been putting in to date. This is also for those that have been working tirelessly on a goal or project and have yet to see any kind of reward. Your frustration is understandable, but you're asked to have faith and know that it's coming. Your hard work has never gone unnoticed by the Universe and Heaven.

You're also asked to take pause if you've been working hard so that you don't experience burn out. When you take a moment to stop and retreat, then you'll come up with a light bulb idea that brings everything all into fruition. You are in tune and in contact with the Divine when you move into the space of stillness. This is where you're able to communicate with your guides more readily as you're paying full attention. They could give you that missing piece needed that gives you the big sell. Your Spirit team is always communicating with you, but are you listening? Not when you're busying away, distracted, or stressing out.

In love, this is also a good card as it can mean that if you're in a relationship that has been disappointing that you both may get a second wind that improves it. Put in the effort to build the connection and blessings will grow out of that.

If you're single and frustrated that there haven't been any potentials, then this is a reminder to stay positive as love is on its way. When you take pause you're able to come to the wisdom or guidance that can help you. You may get a spirit nudge to go to a specific location and not know why. When you head to that location, then you find that you meet the new partner there. If you're in a relationship that is having constant problems, then you may get that official confirmation on whether or not to work at it or throw in the towel indefinitely. If you've been putting in an effort, then this can be saying to keep on trucking because the next partner is coming. There are just temporarily delays or roadblocks in the way at this time. Puzzle pieces might need to be maneuvered to make it happen.

This can also advise to take time out to reflect on what it is you want. There's no rush and this is not a race. Relax and take some time for yourself, preferably in nature to connect. This can be about someone who has started their own business and is concerned that it won't be successful. They've been trying everything, but nothing is working. The Seven of Pentacles is a reminder that you've done a great job at building your business. Success is up ahead so have no fear and keep going. This same concept can be applied to a love relationship as well as other areas.

In the end, the Seven of Pentacles is a message that any hard work you've been putting into what you desire is on its way. Your efforts have not gone unnoticed even if it feels like it at the time. Keep going and do what you've been doing because you're on the right track!

Eight of Pentacles

*T*he Eight of Pentacles in a reading shows someone who is hard at work perfecting their craft. They are enjoying what they're working on. The message can be suggesting that you need to do some additional research surrounding what it is you desire. If it's a particular job you want, then work on perfecting your resume, gain extra knowledge in the genre, or study up on the company and its history. If you want to write a book on a particular topic, then this shows that you'll need to dive heavily into research on that particular genre. You may need to get your feet wet through hands on methods. This doesn't mean if it's a book on serial killers that you partake in the act, but if it's a book on pottery, then take a class on it even if you already know how to do it. The point is to get your mind into that head space of the topic. This can be suggesting that you take a class in the area of your interest.

The Eight of Pentacles is all about acquiring an additional skill, or that one would be needed in reference to the question. You will be that much stronger for it.

This might also suggest that your next job role will be in an area you might not have much knowledge about. As a result, you'll walk away from the job having learned this new skill and talent you did not have before.

The Eight of Pentacles shows a hard working employee that any company would be lucky to have on their staff. This might be an internship or a new job coming up. It could be saying that you should consider turning your passion into a self-employment business that makes you money so that you won't have to work a day job you have no interest in. This can also show that you are already working away at your self-employment business, but you haven't reached that point where you are able to quit your day job in order to focus on it full time. The Eight of Pentacles is a sign that you are heading in that direction, so keep going since successful self-employment is near.

This represents someone who is great at what they do. They enjoy this passion so much that it's difficult to pull them away from it. They could be working long hours and late into the night for the pure enjoyment of this work because it doesn't feel like work to them. This is work you would do for free because you enjoy it.

Typically, the image in the traditional card shows a figure hard at work hammering a pentacle, but there are several other pentacles that have been pinned up which shows he's finished some of the work and still plugging away tirelessly and diligently. He's not distracted, but focused and concentrated. This is someone who is great at their job. If there is something you desire, the Eight of Pentacles says you will need to put in work and effort to get it. It's not going to land in your lap by doing nothing.

In a love relationship reading, this might be showing that your potential partner or current lover has been busy and hard at work. This could be why they haven't surfaced yet or paid much attention to you. They're merely consumed by work at the moment.

The Eight of Pentacles might be saying that you could meet your partner while taking a class or diving into the trade of your interest. This is where you bump into the new person. It might also be saying that you gain and learn new positive traits by being around this person or they will with you. The both of you gain while being in one another's presence. This can be a teacher-student relationship dynamic where there is much to teach and learn from the other. You both bring something that the other might not have knowledge around. This message also might be saying you need to gain a little more dating experience before the lifelong partner surfaces.

The potential personality trait of the Eight of Pentacles person is that they value long term relationships. They will work to keep a relationship thriving because they understand the value of it. This will come naturally for them, but you would need to be the same way in order for it to keep going.

If this is about a love relationship in general, then this shows a couple that works on their union together. If you've been having issues or discord with a partner, then the Eight of Pentacles says to work together through compromise by bringing peace to the connection. Work on the connection together in order to resolve any issues.

In the end, the Eight of Pentacles is about putting in the effort, or continue working in the direction you've been in as what you desire will be reached if you keep going.

Nine of Pentacles

*T*he Nine of Pentacles message can point to being financially independent or that it's on the way. This is a great card to get for someone who is desiring to be self-employed, as it shows you being successful at it. If you're already self-employed, then this can say that it will continue to grow and be successful. You are in a position where you are completely independent on all levels.

The Nine of Pentacles is also someone who doesn't need anyone. They're not desiring to be attached to anything or anyone. This person doesn't need or require praise from outsiders. They can do their work through the pure love and joy of it. Any praise that comes for a person like this is appreciated, but not required in any manner that fulfills them. They will do their work regardless of praise or fanfare.

In the previous Eight of Pentacles card, it showed someone working tirelessly at their craft, but the Nine of Pentacles shows they've officially completed and excelled at their craft. The rewards have filtered in with the Nine of Pentacles. This is someone that can take a long break if they choose and enjoy the luxuries or riches they've accumulated. This is the financial gain card for someone's hard work implemented in the previous Eight of Pentacles card.

The Nine of Pentacles in love shows an emotionally detached

person in a relationship. They are strong, loyal, and financially independent, but they are not co-dependent when it comes to having a partner. They can be alone and be perfectly content. This can be someone who also might not have a huge social life or require one. They don't get lonely the way others might after no human contact. They are self-made, confident, and not requiring constant attention from external sources.

The Nine of Pentacles can show someone who values a relationship with you, but they don't need to be around you 24/7. This can be a relationship where two people have separate lives or who live in separate residences, but every now and then they get together or go out on a date. They are loyal to one another even if they see each other infrequently.

The Nine of Pentacles can be a positive card for some love relationships. It reveals a couple who are independent and level headed. They've achieved their dreams and have time to enjoy one another. They both like their personal freedom. This doesn't mean free to stray and date other people. On the contrary, you're much involved with each other, loyal, and devoted. You love the security and safety of the relationship. You may live together, but half the time you do your own thing and the other half you join in to do things together. This couple is not the type who are constantly joined at the hip and only doing things if both agree on it.

If this is about a potential partner, then it could show the person using self-restraint or holding back. This is not necessarily out of caution or restraint, which would be the Four of Pentacles. They may be into you in a romantic way, but they're extremely level headed and patient when it comes to love.

This card can also reveal someone who has everything in their life except a love partner. If you're asking about a potential, then this can show that the person you're asking about is ready for love. They are in a position to receive it and will be loyal and constant while in it.

This is a successful put together person who has achieved quite a bit in their life. They might have the fat resume, credentials, or financially secure bank account, but their personality is on an even keel. This is someone who rarely gets angry, but they can be cold and tough when pushed to anger. They offer a cool glare and everyone knows they mean business. The Nine of Pentacles wants the bullet points and then have everyone move on. Think of the character Miranda Priestly in *the Devil Wears Prada* to match the image of the Nine of Pentacles.

Incidentally, on a general level the message in this card can be advising you to use self-restraint or detachment surrounding a situation. If you've been emotionally erratic about something, then this card is the message that says maintain equilibrium. Use calm refined togetherness in all of your dealings and endeavors.

Ten of Pentacles

*T*he Ten of Pentacles is one of the most positive cards in the Pentacles suit. This shows someone who has unlimited stability from the wonderful career, home, love relationship, and family, or circle of close ones. If they don't yet, then this is a positive indicator that they are heading in that direction.

With the Seven of Pentacles, you were planting the seeds of your desires waiting for results. The Eight of Pentacles revealed you hard at work becoming exceptional at your craft. The Nine of Pentacles saw the bearing of those seeds bringing in abundance for your hard work, but the Ten of Pentacles shows you being content with where you are at. You are in a place to invite in a love partner and build a life together.

This is the strong foundation and security card. One has reached a high level of success in some area of their life. This can indicate great financial flow, inheritance, gambling winnings, or other means of abundance coming into your life. This can be the buying or selling of a house, property, or a new apartment move. This is taking one's life to the next practical level where one obtains the home, career, and marriage partner. In general, it's an overall sense of positive well-being, security, and happiness.

If you were worried about money, this would indicate that your money issues are over. The Ten of Pentacles can also be about seeking security in a situation or circumstance. This is someone needing more stability in their life. This might also be a conservative person in some area, whether that be financially or with their personal ethics, values, and code of conduct. This person is a strong, stable, disciplined, and solid character who values traditionalism and enjoys some measure of order. You can count on this person to last and be loyal and honest.

This is one of the great cards to receive surrounding whatever it is you desire. For love, it can indicate moving in together or a stronger commitment with a love partner. This is a couple who has reached contentment as a union. They are a power couple who excel at everything they do.

In a love relationship, this card would show a big yes that the next love partner is coming, and they are likely the one you stay with for life. It might show this person as being marriage material and at a place where they desire the same things you want. You will move in together and build a strong security based life.

Security, success, and stability in the practical world is the basis of this card. The marriage partner might be wealthy or financially secure. They also desire a long term marriage partner and deep commitment that endures the through the end of your lives. This can also point to someone who has reached some kind of high status, social standing, or position in life. This includes moving into a higher level spiritually while moving along your Earthly journey.

Page of Pentacles

PAGE of PENTACLES.

PERSON:

The Page of Pentacles can reveal a young person around or under 25 who has an Earth sign in the top tier of their chart. This is Taurus, Virgo, Capricorn. *(Top tier can be Sun sign, Rising, Moon, Venus, Mars)*

If they do not have those stats, then this is someone regardless of age or sign who is slow moving, but one of the more grounded mature Pages. They move slowly, but achieve beyond measure. They have a steady plodding energy.

This is someone who is interested in study and diving into intellectual pursuits. They have a focus on building security from an early age where they are already thinking about and planning for their future. They're the young person found reading a book, or they're at a bookstore, library, or taking a class.

This is also someone who is an apprentice or a novice at a particular craft. It might be used to describe you with this book! You are gradually perfecting the craft of an area of interest by diving into research and hands on methods in order to gain additional knowledge. This is the general Page of Pentacles message.

MESSENGER:

Will the person I have an interest in contact me? The message with the Page of Pentacles is they will contact you, but the answer is 'eventually'. They move slowly and are in no rush to contact. It's not like the Page of Wands who contacts impulsively, and then perhaps changes their mind, or blows out of there just as quickly. The Page of Pentacles contacts when the time is right. They are methodical in their approach and may already know in the back of their mind that they will be contacting you, but when they get around to it. They might be studying you up to make sure it's safe to proceed. They are the one Page that is in it for the long haul despite how young they might seem. They appreciate solid together people who value loyalty and building something that lasts. When they do contact, it's to gradually build longevity and security.

This person loves going to school, taking a class, or higher learning. They are seen studying up and researching things even if just for fun. They are typically a quiet reserved person, but not necessarily shy. They're not into partying and may only partake in it once in a blue moon or if a friend drags them. It doesn't excite their level headedness to get sloshed. They'd rather have intellectual banter at a coffee house. This may be an animal lover who enjoys building or using their hands in some way. They are usually a practical person in all ways with relaxed casual clothing, jeans/shorts/t-shirts/flip-flops.

Where the Page of Wands loves tons of people around, the Page of Pentacles prefers to be alone or with a close trustworthy friend or two. The Page of Pentacles can also present positive news pertaining to school, life lessons, or finances.

SITUATION:

The Page of Pentacles in a reading can indicate the start of a new job. It can say that any money making endeavors are off to a good start. This doesn't show huge financial abundance, but this is someone who makes enough to survive with a little cushion to spend on themselves. This person will need to budget so they don't go overboard.

The traditional image of this card shows a young person holding one pentacle or coin in their hand. They have made their first monies and are holding onto it proudly to say, "See what I've earned?" They have a sense of security. How should they spend it or perhaps it's better to invest or save it? It's not a lot, but it is just enough that gives them a feeling that things are looking up on the security front.

The Page of Pentacles can also show some positive news coming in surrounding work or finance opportunities. This is about being practical, realistic, and budget conscious. It can be about finding ways to build your finances and the possible avenues that can assist with that. It may be telling you to consider getting a job if you don't work, or find something productive to dive into for supplemental income.

This can also be about partaking in grounding physical exercise such as a running, biking, or climbing. It can indicate the start of good health if you were previously suffering in any way.

Like the tortoise and the hare, the tortoise is like the Page of Pentacles. They may start out slow that it seems as if they'll finish in last place, but in the end they end up winning the race!

The Page of Pentacles can be the start of a physical long lasting relationship. This is a slow moving connection that gradually grows stronger over the months and years. At first it seems as if nothing is really going on with it, but when one looks back in hindsight, the connection is lasting longer than any other.

The Page of Pentacles is a friends first before anything else kind of a relationship. Will you reunite with an ex? Page of Pentacles can indicate slow steady improvement that may take a long while before results are seen. The ultimate message is slow gradual moving towards something substantial in some area of your life.

Knight of Pentacles

KNIGHT of PENTACLES

PERSON:

    The Knight of Pentacles can reveal a person around 25-35 who has an Earth sign in the top tier of their chart. This is Taurus, Virgo, Capricorn. *(Top tier can be Sun sign, Rising, Moon, Venus, Mars)*

    If they do not have those stats, then this is someone regardless of age or sign who is protective, loyal, and grounded. They are someone who is into building for the future. They are the mellowest of all four Knights in the Tarot. They are methodical and exacting while carefully planning their next move before they even make the move. The Knight of Wands is impulsive and sometimes reckless in their moves, while the Knight of Pentacles takes its time. He is moving towards his goal even if it seems as if he's standing still. He is applying more towards it than one might realize.

    The challenging side can be they move too slow in making a decision that they can miss an opportunity. In the end, the Knight of Pentacles is protective of those they love and of themselves. Accumulating wealth to them is important as it gives them a sense of security. They would rather be their own boss or run their own company than be a willing follower. They might not be fully ready for a relationship as they haven't quite reached the height of their dreams the way the King of Pentacles has. They are in the middle of working away to reach that level.

If you're looking for longevity and romance, then the Knight of Pentacles and the Knight of Cups are your Knights. The Knight of Pentacles may not quite be in a place where they are ready for a relationship even if they're thinking of one. This Knight is not as established as the King and still struggling to make it. This may take precedence over a relationship. If you're easy-pleasy and this doesn't bother you that you'll hardly see them, then standing by them will let them know you have what it takes to last a lifetime with them. They cherish loyalty and respect in others because they have this in spades. This Knight of Pentacles is on the conservative side and prefers tradition and structure to chaos and unplanned events.

SITUATION:

The Knight of Pentacles in a reading might be someone who is stubborn or unwavering on an issue. This might be good or bad depending on the context of the question. If it's a love relationship, then someone would welcome someone they desire coming after them without ever giving up.

This can also be asking you to move with caution and don't rush into anything. Take your time, double check all sides, weigh the pros and cons. In a work reading, this can show you as being hardworking and productive to the point that whatever you desire to achieve in career related endeavors that you do have what it takes.

The typical image of the Knight of Pentacles shows him sitting on his horse not moving as opposed to the Knight of Wands and Knight of Swords who are dashing through the fields. This doesn't necessarily mean that nothing is happening, but in fact the opposite. This Knight is observing his surroundings as he gradually moves forward. He's taking the time to look for all the trap doors that could be a problem and waiting until it's safe to proceed. If you've been patient in hoping something will happen in an area of your life, the Knight of Pentacles shows positive movement is forthcoming even if it doesn't seem like it at the moment. The Knight is coming, but just taking its time. The same goes for business success. Be ambitious and continue building and then you will see results.

This can show someone who blends into the wall, so it can be asking you to come out of your comfort zone and let yourself be seen. This is not someone who is a big talker unless they are expounding about a topic they know quite a bit about. The Knight of Pentacles can be possessive about all of their material and physical blessings accumulated. This includes a romantic partner who they also may see as a possession.

Queen of Pentacles

QUEEN of PENTACLES

PERSON:

The Queen of Pentacles can reveal someone around aged 35 and above who has an Earth sign in the top tier of their chart. This is Taurus, Virgo, Capricorn. *(Top tier can be Sun sign, Rising, Moon, Venus, Mars)*

If they do not have those stats, then this is someone regardless of age or sign who is a balanced hardworking person. They may be quietly working calmly only to throw others off by how far they've climbed up the ladder. This person attracts in success through hard work, but they are rarely rattled and are grounded, stable, and put together. This person can balance home and work life with amazing gusto. They appreciate stability and enjoy having a disciplined routine. They are also generous to those close to them or who they trust.

Speaking of trust, it can take the Queen of Pentacles awhile to come around with someone new as they have to gain that persons trust gradually over time. They are not instant friends with anybody even though they can be friendly. This can also be an animal lover who has a big heart. They may appreciate animals more than people for that matter.

While this person is great at their career and may love their job, this is mostly due to the security it provides. This person is generally super domesticated and loves being at home rather than going out. They also have an open door policy that welcomes others with a smile. They are always having people pop by where they make that person feel at home by entertaining and feeding them. When they do go out, they tend to frequent nature spots or they meet the neighbors in order to rally them altogether in positive community. It can take time to get close to this person, but when the Queen of Pentacles comes around they make a lifelong best friend. This can also indicate a best friendship with someone who could be a friend, family member, colleague, or lover.

SITUATION:

The Queen of Pentacles in a situation reading can show abundance and prosperity flowing into your life surrounding the question that was asked. This is about being resourceful and accumulating all of the tools you need to make something happen. This can include polishing up your resume and researching the ins and outs of companies that interest you and catch your eye.

In love relationships, this can show a trustworthy connection between two people that might start off as friends first. This is a great card to get for someone looking for a long term love relationship as this can reveal a connection that is a solid, secure, loving, and long term committed oriented one. This may also suggest that you need to be a friend to someone first, or that the potential partner is someone who starts out as a friendship. While in a relationship, this is the kind of connection where they seem to do everything together.

The Queen of Pentacles says you have what it takes to achieve your desires. If you keep at it, then you will get it. This message is a positive one that abundance is or will be flowing to you.

King of Pentacles

KING of PENTACLES.

PERSON:

The King of Pentacles can reveal someone around aged 35 and above who has an Earth sign in the top tier of their chart. This is Taurus, Virgo, Capricorn. *(Top tier can be Sun sign, Rising, Moon, Venus, Mars)*

If they do not have those stats, then this is someone regardless of age or sign who is financially secure, stable, and together in all ways. They are a grounded person who might be married to their job or they run their own company. They are interested in accumulating wealth. This is not to be rich for the sake of being rich, but to ensure lifelong security. They find joy in being comfortable in their secure lives with an equally secure mate. They tend to take care of themselves inside and out as much as possible as well too.

As a mate, they are the marriage partner that can last a lifetime. They have a passionate side that comes out with an attentive loyal partner. They value this loyalty and commitment and require it with any potentials they have their eyes on. If they notice those traits lacking in someone, then they will move along. This person is generous and charitable with their fortune to those less fortunate.

This is someone who takes his time building, so he's not going to jump into a relationship at the drop of the hat. He prefers the slow build to something that lasts forever. The same goes for his work and business endeavors. He's more patient than the King of Wands and will stand by a deal when the King of Wands might recklessly dump it at the slightest moment.

On the challenging side, the King of Pentacles can be stubborn unwilling to make a decision that needs to be made quickly. They may not commit right away until their ready. They also won't budge on something that should be let go. However, when they do commit to someone or something, they look at it as being until the end of their lives.

SITUATION:

The King of Pentacles is much like the Ten of Pentacles card where one obtains abundance that brings in security whether that is an uptick in finances, the house, job, career, or solid relationship. The King of Pentacles is a super positive card to get in terms of relationship commitment, because it shows someone who is steadfast. It reveals a connection that is grounded and facing the same direction where both parties desire something long term. In business, this shows someone who is established and not struggling to make it. They have already achieved what they desire and are merely working to maintain it.

The King of Pentacles puts in hard work and dedication to all of his endeavors, so this is what is asked of you should this card come up. It can also show financial security flowing to you if it hasn't been.

If you're single, then this can show you coming across a potential partner who is stable and grounded. They might be slow moving, but in the end they are the keeper as they're able to go the distance. They may lack a little spontaneity and adventure, but those types are not usually known for sticking around in the end. The King of Pentacles shows a solid connection with mutual respect and admiration. This person prefers a sabbatical hike in nature rather than heading out to a nightclub or bar.

In a love relationship, this can show a couple who is on an equal footing where they both value commitment and security. They work together to ensure the connection is strong and long lasting. On a challenging note, this might show a couple that isn't exactly direct and verbal about their feelings. They tend to show how they feel through their actions such as taking you away for a weekend getaway or buying you 'things' they think you might like. The King of Pentacles can be asking you to be more verbal in your communication or to work on being more loyal, grounded, and stable.

Cups/Water

The Cups suit in the Tarot is one of my favorite suits because it's focus is on love, relationships, and emotions. You can be asking the Tarot a question about love and receive cards in another suit, but it doesn't make that any less valuable. However, the Cups suit is where the feelings and relationship needs are. This still applies to work, career, or any other part of your life, but it is heavier up on emotions and connections. The Cups suit could reveal feelings associated with a job or whatever the question is if it is outside of love. Where the Swords suit focuses on thinking processes, the Cups suit focuses on thinking with one's feelings. Whether you're keeping the emotions contained or letting it loose. The Cups is the last suit were looking at in this as I wanted to wrap up with love and relationships. It is love after all that makes the world thrive. Love has the power to banish away any seeming darkness. There isn't enough love in the world to begin with.

Ace of Cups

ACE of CUPS.

*T*he Ace of Cups is a bright and cheery card in a reading that shows the beginnings of a situation that brings one positive feelings of joy. This can be asking you to be open to receive love or telling you that a new relationship love partner is on the horizon. Surrender to it and allow it to carry you away. This card can also indicate strong psychic intuition and to pay attention to that. This promises good circumstances on the horizon that bring you an uplifting feeling. It can also be about merging creativity and intuition to create striking work that emotes strong feelings in others.

The Ace of Cups might show a new opportunity or work situation that will bring you emotional fulfillment. It can also reveal optimistic promise with a new person you're dating. It is only showing the beginnings of that promise. The future might be a question mark, but it's already off to a wonderful start, so things are looking good so far. This can also show a romantic date with someone of interest. A mutual fun-loving good time with them is indicated.

This is the intimate, loving, and passionate kind of love. This might be that two people are beginning to open up about their feelings and interest in one another.

The typical image of this card shows one hand holding a huge cup with water flowing out of it. This is about feelings overflowing and filling you up completely.

If one is already in a relationship, then this can show a renewed love or a situation that bonds and brings the couple together positively even more. If there was conflict or discord, then this shows that there will be a miraculous turnaround. It can bring a couple back into the throes of love with good times that surround that. Sometimes this is seen in tempestuous connections where the couple seem to be passionately in love one minute, then at odds the next, then in love, and so forth. This can also apply to other connections whether it's a friend, colleague, or family member one is having trouble with.

This is also the forgiveness card. If you were having trouble with someone, then this is saying to bury the hatchet and forgive them. It's time to let go of any animosity and allow your love light to shine on them. Extend the olive branch and make peace.

In general, the Ace of Cups can be asking you to open up more. Perhaps you are reserved, introverted, or guarded. This would be advising you that it's time to work on being more open. On a spiritual level, this message can point to psychic insight, premonitions, or the beginnings of evolving spiritually.

This could say that there is a new move of residence coming. It might be with a romantic partner, or you meet someone new after you move. If you're already in a relationship, it can be a renewed feeling of love in the current relationship.

If you asked a work related question, then this is a good sign that there is a promotion up ahead or a new job altogether. It is something that brings you delight and satisfaction.

Because this card is the birth of something that brings emotional fulfillment, it can also be an actual birth or a pregnancy. This is literally or metaphorically, such as a baby or the birth of a creative project. It can also be to infuse more feeling into your work or relationship. This message is also about you having a positive spiritual awakening or to honor self-love and self-care. Do something for you that brings you joy and contentment.

The Ace of Cups is a new beginning connected to something that brings an emotional uplifting feeling, whether it's a pregnancy, start of a creative project, job, romance, spiritual growth, or the awakening of psychic perception. It is also the start of a new love that has the potential to be the one that becomes the marriage partner, or a renewed sense of love with a current lover.

Ace of Cups heralds a new relationship with passion, excitement and happiness. This is a positive card to get for love as it shows beautiful promise.

Two of Cups

With the Ace of Cups, you saw the start of a potential romance that revealed something kinetic. Where will it go and how far will it go? The Two of Cups shows the connection growing deeper, closer, and more loving. The Two of Cups is a card that many are happy to see in a reading when looking for romance.

If you were single and asking if a love relationship is coming, then this card is a positive sign that yes it is! It bypasses the Ace of Cups and hits the intimate loving bond almost immediately. Whereas the Ace of Cups is usually the beginnings of a love relationship or a fun romantic time, the Two of Cups shows a couple that feels as if they've known each other for lifetimes. They immediately hit it off as if they're picking up where they originally left off. The Two of Cups can say that you will have a close loving relationship tie with this person. It can also indicate a stronger commitment with someone you are dating.

The Two of Cups will show a dating situation moving up to the next level, which is romantic relationship. This is the true love card that reveals being in the happy honeymoon phase of a connection. It's also the card that indicates two people that are an inseparable mirror of each other. This is regardless if it's love, friendship, family member, or colleague. This is the platonic kind of relationship of two people uniting or joining together. This is also both a romantic and sexual attraction in a love reading. It may also show a soul mate or twin flame relationship. One negative about this card is if you were looking to see if someone you had your eye on was dating someone else, then the Two of Cups turned over could show they are deeply in love with another person. Look to other cards to see how that will go.

If you're already in a love relationship, then this can be asking the two of you to compromise and meet half way. This is especially the case if there have been issues. The Two of Cups can show the rift being smoothed out as you move back to a deeper bond.

In work, this can show the merging or joining with another team member. The work relationship is fulfilling emotionally for both people. It can reveal a bond that moves into a tighter friendship or a positive working connection.

The Two of Cups is one of the more joyful cards in the Cups suit let alone in the Tarot. Those who see this card pop up in a reading for them tend to smile or breathe a sigh of relief.

The Two of Cups can also reveal a deep best friendship. This is one that might start at a level where they are two peas in a pod. They go the distance and endure a lifetime together as Best Friends Forever. This is about joining forces with another person in a positive welcoming way.

Ultimately, the Two of Cups indicates a marriage or a stronger deeper commitment with someone. It may also reveal a business contract or merging between you and another on a work level whether it's a new job or a new business you're starting. The Two of Cups reveals that whatever question you've asked, it will be emotionally satisfying and gratifying for you.

Three of Cups

*T*he Three of Cups points to friendships with others, social fun, or some kind of celebration. It can indicate a good time or a social event.

This is the card that shows someone who is tons of fun, exuberant, cheery, full of life, and positive energy. When they walk in a room, everyone notices and is excited to see them. This is a popular person who isn't afraid to put themselves out there. If you were previously sad, glum, depressed or any other negative emotion, the Three of Cups shows an influx of positive feelings and experiences on the horizon.

If one is a loner type, then this card can be advising you to get out there and socialize. Find a social circle with similar interests by researching groups that enjoy hobbies that you love doing. It can also be to pay attention to events that you're invited to as a potential love interest may be there if you're single. This can include joining groups online if that is easier for you, but let people get to know you in person too.

At work, the Three of Cups shows you being part of a team that gets along exceptionally well working together. You become close friends during the process of working as a team, even if it doesn't continue when you leave this job or project. This is an emotionally satisfying team that works together. They have fun going into work.

In a love relationship, the Three of Cups may not be the most romantic card, but it does have some level of romanticism. It can show an engagement between lovers. It might show a couple that is the best of friends always having a good time with each other. It might be the kind of relationship that is always busy entertaining friends at home. There is always someone popping by at this household. The Two of Cups pointed to love relationships, but the Three of Cups points strongly to friendships, so it can be romantic couple who are also each other's best friends.

If you're currently in a relationship, then this can be that a stronger commitment is coming like a marriage or civil union. It can be asking you both to inject more fun into your union, go out and do something fun together. Have date night once a week or throw a party or gathering with friends or family.

The Three of Cups can be a challenging card as well depending on the surrounding cards. If it shows up next to the Seven of Swords for example, then it may show that there is a third party in the mix. Infidelity or betrayal of some kind. If there are court cards around, then that can further indicate if there is cheating or a lack of loyalty going on. This can also be the case if the card falls out of the deck upside down or happens to be flipped over reversed.

If you're wondering if you and someone will get together in a dating set up, then this can point to it being a deep fun friendship with the possibility of more. It is friendship first before anything else. In the end, it is someone you will enjoy and vice versa. In business, this can show an alliance or happily working with others. It can say promote and market yourself! Celebrate all that you are and get out there!

If you want to know how a potential sees you, then the Three of Cups can show that they see you as a best friendship that they love, but they may not necessarily have romantic feelings or want a relationship with you. It can also be advising you to enjoy the moment and avoid dissecting what you and this other person are or could become.

The Three of Cups points to positive teamwork, camaraderie, friendships, being of high spirits, social events, and community. The message in the card describes someone who is so happy they feel like dancing or singing. It can also show a good time at a concert or a date. It doesn't necessarily say it will stand the test of time, but it does show two people who enjoy being in one another's company.

In the end, the Three of Cups shows a stronger connection with someone, a friendship, or fun times. It may also show a marriage proposal or some sort of invitation to a celebratory event that could be a wedding, school, family get together, or reunion.

Four of Cups

*T*he Four of Cups can reveal you to be taking the blessings you have for granted. It can show you as having your heart closed to others. It doesn't mean you don't feel or have empathy for them, when in fact it's quite the opposite. You might have a casing or wall around your heart unable to see the good that is around you. You have fallen into hyper self-analysis of your own feelings. You are deeply focused on your emotions and needs to the point that you are not seeing there are blessings, miracles, and answered prayers to your desires around you. If you would lift your head up and pay attention, then you would notice the good.

The Four of Cups asks you to have more gratitude and notice that there are gifts, answers, blessings, and good things around you if you would pay attention to see it.

This might also be seen as a challenging card as it typically shows a figure sitting in the grass with head down feeling low and worthless because their desires are not being met. The message of the card is actually a positive one as the Four of Cups says to lift your head up to notice that what you want is there and within reach. Stop feeling sorry for yourself.

This can also be about needing some time to yourself to figure out your next move. You might be apathetic about your job or relationship and wanting to leave, but unsure how. You need alone time for reflection and insight. This can also show you to be feeling isolated and that you need to come out of hiding and join the world in a positive way.

The Four of Cups can also reveal you to be experiencing boredom. It feels as if your life force is gone. You have no passion, drive, or much interest in anything.

The Four of Cups can say that your Spirit team is working with you. They're revealing steps for you to take by also handing little opportunities that propel you one move closer to your dream. You're so dispirited that you're not noticing it. Get happy and be optimistic believing that you have everything you want, then watch your world open up. The message in this card says to elevate your mood when it takes a dip into pessimism.

In a love relationship reading, if you're single then this can show that you're feeling negative emotions that there is no lover, but the Four of Cups says you have much to be grateful for. There is the possibility of a romantic partner connection around you. They might be someone you had never considered. It can be someone who is currently in your vicinity, and super close so pay attention. This can also show you to have given up on love and feeling no point in remaining hopeful that it will happen, even though there is a potential around you that you're not noticing it with all that glumness you're carrying.

If it's a personality trait one is looking at, then the Four of Cups might show that the person may be a nonchalant kind of character. It doesn't mean they're not interested, so don't misread their casual attitude since sometimes that masks how they really feel about you, which could be positive. They may need to be shown that you are into them and do care. They're not noticing you around them or paying attention.

However, this card can also show that a missed opportunity may have passed you by and you've fallen into disappointment and despondence.

There may not be something specific in your life that has caused such unhappiness. You're not seeing the blessings you currently have. You're being handed something awesome, but you're so down that you're not noticing it. Get happy now and look at the bright side of things. If you're currently single and you pull this card, it can be that a romantic suitor is around you, but you're so distracted or down that you don't see this person. This can also show someone that is in a self-absorbed state that they don't recognize anything else.

In a love relationship, this might show someone that has become dissatisfied with the connection. They no longer feel passionate about it and are entertaining thoughts of what to do. It doesn't mean they intend to leave, but this card could present a state of mind about someone that could later kick off their departure if they don't bounce out of that state.

This can also show a partner who is withholding affection out of selfishness or the inability to see how great they have it with someone. It could be a temporary withholding of affection if the couple previously had a fight and the partner was wrongfully hurt. In that case, the withholding can be temporary especially if there are other cards outside of that which indicate all will be well again.

While the Three of Cups had shown good times at a social event or with friends, the Four of Cups shows someone who has become apathetic and indifferent. They're turning down invitations and want to be by themselves now. They don't have any passion left to muster and push themselves to engage with others. This could present a missed opportunity that would be a blessing.

The Four of Cups could also show someone who has stopped putting in an effort into a relationship. Their self-interest can supersede allowing room for another person to enter their vicinity including their partner. They are terribly unhappy with what they have.

Ultimately, the Four of Cups is advising you to get unstuck with your emotions. You're running around in an endless merry go round circle of watery emotions that goes nowhere, but only brings more unhappiness.

The Four of Cups can also show that something unexpected could reveal itself to you. Pay attention to what's around you as there is something you should take notice of.

Five of Cups

*T*he Five of Cups is one of the gloomier cards in the Tarot deck.

It shows someone experiencing depression, sadness, or grief. Usually it's tied to an ending or a loss of some kind, whether it's the end of a relationship, the passing of a loved one, the loss of a job, or any other kind of loss. It can also indicate someone suffering from depression.

When one experiences this kind of loss and grief it is mostly always temporary. Allow yourself to grieve and come to terms with the loss. Nothing lasts forever as every human being will pass on and depart this planet. No one is exempt from upsetting situations in human life. Do your best to work through it in order to not let it drown you in a permanent state of sadness.

The emotional feelings you're experiencing are heavy while creating a fog around the truth. There is no clear perception at this time. Allow the feelings to be felt knowing that the sun will come up and illuminate what you learned from with a loss.

The Five of Cups can also show you saying goodbye to someone. Maybe a friend, lover, or family member was visiting for a couple weeks from out of town. You had such a great time, but now it's time for them to go back home. This hits you hard as they mean the world to you. It can also be the ending of a love relationship and you're in the throes of emotional pain attempting to make sense of the ending. Usually this card indicates that the ending might have come unexpectedly. Perhaps there was a betrayal or they abruptly left leaving you stunned since there were no real signs that anything was wrong. This can also be a lover who is out of town or has been away for awhile. The Five of Cups shows this intense sad longing wishing they were around you.

This card can also show temporary moodiness where nothing is really wrong, but you might be prone to ups and downs with emotion. The Five of Cups could currently show this melancholy. This is also about feeling regret about someone or something. The previous Four of Cups card can show a missed opportunity, but the Five of Cups would show the regret over losing this missed opportunity.

The message can show you to be stuck in the past unable to move forward. Things happen for a reason and in order to move on and rise above any sadness, adjust your thoughts into accepting the situation that has transpired and let it go. Move on from the past and look up ahead on the path that is lit up with possibilities.

In the end, when you consult with the cards on whether or not to pursue a business venture, a major decision, or potential love partner, then the Five of Cups could show disappointment around that. It would instruct that its best to wait or that the end result may bring on unnecessary emotional pain, upset, or sadness.

If you're single, then the Five of Cups can show your current down state of mind, which won't attract in a partner. It may be asking you to get out there, or get happy and accept that there is no partner yet. You may have a bad negative attitude without realizing it. When you change your attitude to something positive, then this can help bring in bright prospects.

This can also show that you have been crossing paths with potentials, but your own down mood are keeping it at bay. Sometimes when it's been so long since you've had a romantic partner, then you might not know how to accept and deal with that when a good one does show up. You end up freezing up or putting off a vibe that you have no interest. Work on conveying a positive attitude while you're out and about.

The Five of Cups is a sad card when it comes to love. It doesn't necessarily show a break up, but it shows that someone is terribly unhappy and down. This isn't the angry kind of unhappy, but the depressed and sad energy. You feel really low like you can't go on. Perhaps you were hurt or disappointed by a current partner. They left you, you left them, or you're sad that you don't have a partner.

The Five of Cups shows deep sadness, but know that nothing stays the same. The sad feelings will eventually evaporate, but you need to take action steps to get there. This can also be about excessive worry to the point that its weighing you down and stalling you from functioning. This can say there is a separation, ending, or divorce. There may be negative feelings around a loss. Someone is mired in the past and upset about it. When this comes up as truth, then work on moving through these sad feelings understanding that there are ups and downs in life. You will not feel this way forever since time heals all wounds.

Six of Cups

*T*he Six of Cups can show you to be in nostalgic mode reminiscing about the past. This isn't the negative emotions surrounding the past that was in the Five of Cups. This is more uplifting, satisfying, and exciting feelings about the past.

The Six of Cups can also be advising you to let loose, let your inner child out to play, and have some fun. It's a message to enjoy yourself and connect with that inner child in you, and the carefree happy attitude you might have had as a child at play.

This card can reveal emotional, happy, harmonic feelings rising to the forefront after a period of disappointment. After the sadness of the Five of Cups and the apathy in the Four of Cups, it is a welcome relief to come to the Six of Cups revealing a renewed spirit for life again. It can also indicate a déjà vu or a blast from the past kind of feeling.

The Six of Cups shows someone with a giving nature who has a childlike wonder about them. They are usually fun loving, compassionate, and bring out the best in others. This can also reveal anything having to do with Children, whether it is having Children, or someone who works with them.

In ones work life, this might be asking you to adopt a more

childlike welcoming attitude with colleagues. This card is also about having a satisfying emotional experience connected to work.

In a love relationship reading, this can show a possible rekindling of a love partnership with an ex or former lover. It can also be a friendship whether now or in the past who surfaces and merges with you in a romantic way. This can also indicate a potential love partner who has a deep past life connection with you.

In a relationship, this can be asking that you and your partner have more fun, get playful, and unleash your inner child with one another.

If you're single, then this can be that you're going to be meeting someone, but it may be someone you've been involved with before. This can also indicate someone who you once knew, currently know, or have previously crossed paths with and didn't realize it. It may be a past life romance where a re-connection this lifetime is going to take place.

Seven of Cups

*T*he Seven of Cups shows confusion, delusion, and choices. This can be that you're caught up in the fantasy of something that isn't real. You believe with full force that something is true, when in fact it's a fantasy in your mind. This could also indicate that there is no clarity with a situation.

The Seven of Cups can also show someone who has several choices and options such as with job prospects or love partners. The Seven of Cups can reveal tons of confusion energy where you cannot figure out which choice to make. You will have to make a choice and it's up to you to make the right one that best suits you. The Seven of Cups card traditionally displays seven cups with various images in those cups. This is to indicate that some of these cups have blessings in them, while the other cups may bring on challenges. This is also why it can be nerve wracking trying to figure out which path or choice to take and then hope for the best.

Temptation can be the message in a Seven of Cups reading. You might be having issues with a lover and feel as if they're not in the relationship with you. The Seven of Cups might show them not necessarily cheating, but being tempted and paying attention to temptations presented to them. Kind of like Adam and Eve in the

Garden of Eden story with them being tempted by the snake. This card can also show that the love partner may be experiencing confusion and not knowing whether or not to stay in the connection. It might be that they don't know what they want. They may have a history of unstable connections that are short lived. This can be someone going through a period of soul searching. This can also apply to you falling into temptations for emotional comfort. If that is the case, then the message is asking you to be aware of it. This is in order to dissolve the addictions, since it can be stalling you from moving forward, or it will have negative repercussions.

If someone is single, the Seven of Cups might show a crush on someone that is not reciprocated, or this says that you have tons of potentials swimming around you. Some of them will make a great partner, but others will only bring challenges, so choose wisely.

In a relationship, the Seven of Cups might show a co-dependent relationship where one or both partners are in the connection for superficial reasons. It can also be a relationship that dives into addictions together. It can be an emotional addiction with drama or alcohol and drugs. If it's nothing like that, then there could be temptation or confusion surrounding the connection. The Seven of Cups may also point to the couple needing to make a decision together about something, but are confused as to which one to go with. As in all of the Minor Arcana cards, sometimes these can be small day-to-day issues that are not a super big deal, but it is heavily on your mind or something you'll need to face.

In the traditional image a figure looks up at seven cups floating in the clouds. This can show someone who is confused, overwhelmed, and unsure. This is because what is being presented to you may not entirely be as it appears. In some Tarot decks the cups are filled with something different than the other cups. If your eye is immediately drawn to one cup in particular, then look at what's in that cup to see what the message can be telling you. In some decks there might be a different color of light emanating out of it. The colors can represent someone's chakra energy. This will help in honing in on the area of confusion or choice that needs to be made.

This card can also show a creative, artistic, and imaginative person. The Seven of Cups can also reveal someone who has a co-dependent addictive personality. This might especially be the case if the card is next to other challenging cards such as the Devil or

Temperance.

The Seven of Cups might show someone who moves through life with their head in the clouds. The positives of this is that it's someone with gifted artistic psychic abilities. Having this dreamy nature can be applied positively through creative projects. You just have to take action since the Seven of Cups can reveal you to be is caught up in a dreamy fantasy life, but you're not doing anything to turn these ideas into action. You're basically sitting around waiting for something to land on your doorstep without putting in the work.

The message in the Seven of Cups can also show overindulging in pleasures to the point of excess. This can be someone who is always partying into the night, or having too much alcohol, or consuming bad foods.

In the end, the Seven of Cups surrounds the themes of confusion, delusion, dreams, creativity, choices, addictions, and temptation.

Eight of Cups

*T*he Eight of Cups indicates moving on from a situation where you feel you have no choice. It might be that you did everything you could to make something work, whether it is a relationship or job, but now it's time to move on. Typically, the Tarot image shows a figure hunched over sadly walking away. You might not necessarily want to leave, but feel you have no choice. This is one of the unhappier cards initially to receive in a spread, but not always. The positive is that even if one walks away in a glum depressed manner not wanting to, they are walking towards something. Look to other cards in the spread that can reveal what you are walking towards. The situation cannot be any worse than you felt it to be before it came to a close.

This can also be about taking off on a spiritual quest and leaving everything in your life behind. You may be seeking answers to the bigger questions in life. This is also leaving previous thought processes or values behind in order to embark into a new chapter with a fresh perspective that is different than before. This is choosing to exit one part of your life in order to start a new one.

This can also indicate a move or moving on from something. The Eight of Cups can show you moving on from a situation you've been unhappy in whether it is a relationship, job, or way of life. If this hasn't happened, then this can also be that you've emotionally left a situation in your mind, even if you haven't physically left just yet. You are entertaining thoughts of moving on from something or someone.

The Eight of Cups is about letting go of the past in order to bring in brighter circumstances. It's also about embarking on a new journey or a different path and abruptly leaving the previous one behind. As a result, this can be that you're also abandoning someone or you're the one abandoned in the process. The situation may have felt hopeless to you and you see no other alternative.

In a relationship, this can show that you or another has emotionally invested into a connection, but stayed in it longer than you should have. You might have been wanting to leave for some time since it no longer fulfills you or you've outgrown the connection. The Eight of Cups can reveal that you will be picking up and leaving. This is one of the more unwelcoming cards when it comes to love in that respect, as it can reveal that the person you're asking about will end up leaving you, or it's in their heart or mind to want to do so. They don't necessarily want to, which is why you see the figure in the card hunched over walking away broken and disappointed. It's not a joyful departing and can indicate feeling torn.

Usually when someone wants to leave a relationship, there will be small signs that may or may not be noticed when you're in the throes of the connection. These are things such as they're not as chatty with you as they once were. They are texting or calling less than they used to. They don't communicate as much, seem distant, or they're starting to arrive late to meet up with you. What would make all of this a red flag is if that is not their typical nature and how they've been with you most of the time. When you go out, they seem to be distant with you, including not walking with you. They stray off when you go out together. Again, what would make this unusual is if they're not usually like that to begin with. This is new behavior that has grown consistent. There are no other other personal factors at hand with them that would give reason for their distance with you. Of course all connections, including the greatest love partnerships, reach periods of struggle or distance between one another. Granting one another regular bouts of independence and space gives strength to a relationship. With the Eight of Cups, this is feeling as if you have to leave the connection for good. You're past the point of no return.

This can also be applied to other situations such as the work place.

The employee doesn't seem to have the passion they once had when they go to work. They are always arriving super late or leaving super early. This isn't once in awhile, but pretty much mostly every day. These are signs that the employee has left the job in their heart and are staying because perhaps they're afraid to leave. It's a paycheck that pays their bills, but it's also killing their life force. When you've reached this state regarding anything and you never bounce out of it, then it's time to think of your livelihood and consider making plans to walk away. It's not fair to anyone involved in the situation to have you in that state. It's also not fair to your own sanity and well-being. The energy taints whatever it touches and affects everyone around, including yourself.

While in some cases the Eight of Cups can show a temporary break, it typically does not show that the partner will come back. The Eight of Cups shows the person has moved on or will be moving on. If there is going to be a renewed love at a later date, then the Ace of Cups or Six of Cups would reveal that. Time may need to pass before you conduct an update reading.

The Eight of Cups can also show someone experiencing anxiety and weariness and they need quiet personal time to re-center. It can also show that healing is taking place or is about to. Healing tends to follow an emotional upheaval. The general message of this card can be telling you that it's time to let go of whatever it is you're asking about. Wrap it up and move on knowing that a new chapter will always follow. It may even be better than you anticipate or imagine!

Nine of Cups

*T*he Nine of Cups is one of the most positive cards to receive in a reading, let alone in the Cups suit. It is the wishes come true card. This is whether it be in love relationships, career, or whatever the question asked was. This is a welcome relief after the confusion and delusions of the Seven of Cups, and the walking away of an unhappy situation with the Eight of Cups.

The Nine of Cups is also about feeling satisfied with the outcome of something. You are surrounded by wonderful uplifting friendships and good times. This can also indicate being bestowed with positive blessings, gifts, and good luck.

This is the raise a glass in celebration card. It's about letting loose and having fun. It's feeling content about where you are now. This can also signify abundance rolling in and that whatever you've been wanting to happen is coming into your life in a big way that will make you happy.

The number nine typically shows completion and the Cups suit is feeling oriented. The Nine of Cups can reveal that any previous difficulties have settled and the rough edges have smoothed out. This indicates positive emotional fulfillment surrounding an issue. You've now achieved what you've been forever dreaming about.

The Nine of Cups shows a positive time up ahead. It's also a reason to celebrate as a chapter closes and a new happy one begins. This can be a project that has been wrapped up. It might be the start of a bright new love relationship that will make you both happy. It will grow close offering emotional fulfillment or a secure content feeling to the couple.

If you're currently in a love relationship, then this can be the card that indicates a conversation that happens between both partners that solidifies the commitment even more making you both happy campers. It can also indicate a marriage proposal or stronger commitment.

This is the big triple yes card that says to go for whatever it is you want as it appears to be a sure thing. This is a sexy card and can reveal a hot couple or prospect. This is about having high self-esteem and confidence. In the end, the Nine of Cups is the big wishes and dreams come true card. It doesn't get any better than this.

Ten of Cups

*T*he Ten of Cups takes the Nine of Cups and doubles that whammy. This is one of the best cards to get in the Cups suit also as it shows exhilaration achieved including fairy tale like happy endings. The Ten of Cups reveals someone who has everything they could ever want. This is a metaphor since there will always be something one would want to go after or excel at, but this is an exceptionally exciting card to receive in a reading.

In general, the Ten of Cups shows the home, the love mate partner for life, the family, the kids, the great career, and the never ending happiness. You're going through a period of enjoying all you could ever hope for on an emotional level.

This is the fairy tale ending come true card. This is having the ultimate emotional balance and freedom. This is also about being in a perfect space of contentment. The Ten of Cups shows someone who appears completely together, solid, carefree, and stable. They have a wisdom beyond their years and a sense of knowing.

The Ten of Cups shows emotional security and coming home to a wonderful family or lover they enjoy. This can reveal one who is reveling in the upbeat and cheery sanctuary from the rest of the world. It can also be about someone who is experiencing incredible joy and happiness. Count your blessings and see all of the good that exists around you. This is extending the olive branch and bringing harmony to a connection. The Ten of Cups can also be similar to the Three of Cups where it can show a happy family gathering.

In a love reading, this is one of the happiest cards to receive as it shows a love relationship that lasts a lifetime. It can reveal a strong bond between you and another. It may indicate marriage, long term commitment, or moving in together.

The message pertaining to work life is that your hard work is paying off or will be. The Ten of Cups shows vibrant radiant health. You couldn't ask for anything more than the good stuff that is connected to this card.

The Ten of Cups surrounds the emotional themes of happy times, contentment, pleasure, cheerfulness, joy, bliss, delight, exhilaration, and ecstasy.

Page of Cups

PAGE of CUPS.

PERSON:

The Page of Cups can reveal a young person around or under 25 who has a Water sign in the top tier of their chart. This is Pisces, Cancer, Scorpio. *(Top tier can be Sun sign, Rising, Moon, Venus, Mars)*

If they do not have those stats, then this is someone regardless of age or sign who is romantic in nature, feeling oriented, and governed by their senses and feelings. They are typically a sensual person or have a seductive allure about them that entices and enraptures others. They are a creative being and may work in the creative arts or desire to.

This person may also be super sensitive to the insensitive. They might take everything personally or you feel that you are walking on egg shells around them as you don't want to rattle them into upset. They are delicate and gentle and require a grounded stable person around them to help them flourish and rise.

MESSENGER:

Will the person contact me? The Page of Cups is the most romantic of all of the Pages, so this is a resounding yes. The Page of Cups indicates someone contacting you with romantic or love filled words that they have an interest in you beyond friendship. They may contact you to ask you out on a date or they are having romantic thoughts about you. This contact would be any of the avenues to contact someone via text, phone, social media, or email.

This card can also indicate positive news surrounding love, a social event, an engagement, wedding, or pregnancy. It's usually news that incites warm upbeat happy feelings. It can be a romantic proposition or indicate someone has romantic feelings, but doesn't mean they'll be acted on.

SITUATION:

The Page of Cups can be asking you to pay attention to your sensitivities and psychic hunches. There is great insight being related to you. This can denote a creative artist and the start of something great in the realms of art and creativity. It can be someone filled with love naturally in an intoxicating high.

In a love relationship, this might ask you to be more attached to someone as the other person may feel you to be distant. It can ask you to follow your heart. This might be about having a deep bonding moment with someone. This can point to you having big dreams that must be put into action.

The Page of Cups can be the start of a romantic relationship. It can be a romantic date or a loving warm night with someone. It doesn't necessarily indicate whether it will go the distance unless other surrounding cards in the reading point to that such as Nine of Cups, Ten of Cups, Ten of Pentacles, Four of Wands, The Lovers. The Page of Cups is a new love experience, positive encounters, events, social outings, events, a romantic proposal, romantic words, a new job proposal, or good news that brings on feelings of joy and ecstasy.

Knight of Cups

KNIGHT of CUPS.

PERSON:

The Knight of Cups can reveal someone around 25-35 who has a Water sign in the top tier of their chart. This is Pisces, Cancer, Scorpio. *(Top tier can be Sun sign, Rising, Moon, Venus, Mars)*

If they do not have those stats, then this is someone regardless of age or sign who is romantic, dreamy, or feeling oriented. This person is like the fairy tale quintessential Knight in shining armor. This Knight is like Shakespeare and Romeo or Juliet writing or reading you sonnets and poetry. Nothing is too cliché or silly for them when it comes to love and romance. They are a romantic at heart, passionate, devoted, and affectionate. This person always seems to be in a relationship or dating someone. If they're not, they are constantly seeking it out or longing for it. They are a natural flirt with charisma. Sometimes others misjudge them to be flirting with them, when in truth this person is like this with everybody.

The typical image in the Tarot shows this Knight holding a cup which symbolizes that he holds his heart in his hand ready to offer it to the right suitor. He is like the Knight of Wands and Knight of Swords where he needs constant stimulation or he'll grow restless and in search of other opportunities and prospects. The difference is he is governed by feelings. As long as his emotions and feelings are stroked, then he'll be more likely to stick around.

Where the Knight of Swords can grow annoyed by emotional scenes, the Knight of Cups is the one that can be pushed to causing emotional scenes. This is the Knight that will confront you to ask who you were talking to. If they feel there is cause for suspicion, they will create a melodramatic scene and then will gallop gallantly off to someone who appreciates his affections. As long as this Knight feels loved up and supported, he can go the distance. Cut off the love supply and you suffocate his nature. He'll be off in search of warmer loyal conquests. Where the Knight of Swords is ruled by mind, the Knight of Cups is ruled by heart.

SITUATION:

The Knight of Cups in a love reading is a big yes to love coming your way. This can also show someone longing for a love relationship. If you've been too reserved or cautious, then this message is asking you to be more open, loving, and receptive. This may be showing you going through a creative inspirational period. This Knight brings on psychic insight and perceptions. The Knight of Cups can also be pointing to water activities for sport such as swimming.

This may also show an invitation to an event that will bring you emotional fulfillment. It can show a romantic tryst, love related proposal, or gift of some kind that is along the lines of love.

The Knight of Cups in a reading can also be telling you to nurture your dreams and shift them into action. You have a gift and it's time to do something about it and make it a reality. Start taking daily steps towards your goals even if it's just a little bit each day. The Knight of Cups is having big dreams, but when you turn them into a reality, then you've reached the King of Cups.

The Knight of Cups points to love relationships as well as a tendency to feeling overly dramatic, moody, or emotional. Pay attention to some of the social functions you're invited to that you may typically turn down, scoff, or make excuses that you're too tired to go to. Get out of your routine and go. There may be a big possibility that there will be someone there that gets your heart thumping.

The Knight of Cups is the Don Juan Casanova. He is a hardcore romantic and always in love with love, but be careful as sometimes this

Knights emotions can take over. You don't want to drown into too much watery emotion.

If you're already in a relationship, this Knight wants to keep the magic of love and romance alive. It's about that time to add some more sparks to your union if it's been feeling stale lately. Do something that gets the feelings and emotions going in a positive way. Examples: Candlelit dinners, a road trip outing to a naturesque locale, or cuddle up watching old movies.

Queen of Cups

QUEEN of CUPS.

PERSON:

The Queen of Cups can reveal someone around aged 35 and above who has a Water sign in the top tier of their chart. This is Pisces, Cancer, Scorpio. *(Top tier can be Sun sign, Rising, Moon, Venus, Mars)*

If they do not have those stats, then this is someone regardless of age or sign who is extremely sensitive. They are psychically in tune and sense every nuance around them. This person makes an exceptional healer, counselor, or compassionate teacher. Because of this persons heightened sensitivities, they are usually better with one on one situations than being in groups. They retreat within themselves quite a bit and need tons of alone time to gather strength.

This person is super empathic with shifting moods and a vastly creative inner world. They know when something is wrong with someone and therefore they are the first to offer a listening ear. If someone were interested in them romantically, they might find this person standoffish or difficult to get close to, but that's because the Queen of Cups guards her emotions and heart.

Because this person can get hurt easily, the Queen of Cups needs to know you are true and constant. You will have to continuously work her to attract her in. She is loyal, loving, and devoted once she's been won over. The Queen of Cups operates with intuition and inner feelings first while having keen insight into the human condition.

SITUATION:

The Queen of Cups in a reading can be asking you to have more compassion and walk in others shoes without judgment. Trust your intuition surrounding a circumstance. This can also indicate someone with high psychic perception. If that's not you, then it's asking you to work on awakening that through study, since you have the gift as all souls do. In this case, your psychic gifts are especially strong.

This can be about following your heart on a situation. It is also having an understanding of others and revealing more sensitivity. This card can point to gaining emotional security with another or it is you who offers this trait to others.

The Queen of Cups can be asking you to dive into artistic hobbies to awaken your creative spirit. This is about self-expression and being confident with your own feelings. In love, this can show a flirtation in a love connection that has the potential to grow into more if you're single, or it will strengthen a current love partnership.

In a love relationship, this points to a loyal, loving, and faithful pairing. It's one where both intuit and understand one another offering kind reciprocated compassion.

King of Cups

KING of CUPS.

PERSON:

The King of Cups can reveal someone around aged 35 and above who has a Water sign in the top tier of their chart. This is Pisces, Cancer, Scorpio. *(Top tier can be Sun sign, Rising, Moon, Venus, Mars)*

If they do not have those stats, then this is someone regardless of age or sign who is a compassionate healer, teacher, writer, or guide. This is the father figure that all flock to for guidance. The King of Cups is a master at coming to the truth through great insight. While the King of Swords is governed by thoughts, the King of Cups is governed by feelings, except his feelings are controlled most of the time. He has mastered the art of remaining in control, but you don't want to get on his bad side as a hellish fury of ice will come darting at you. He will freeze you out like nobody's business.

In general, the King of Cups is a peaceful person who is emotionally fulfilled and offers that emotional fulfillment in return. People tend to flock to the King of Cups for his warmth, strength, loving nature, and keen insight.

The King of Cups is one of the more popular Kings in social circles because of his charming debonair personable nature. While the King of Wands can bring on sunshine and liven up an atmosphere, the

King of Wands doesn't have much time to listen to the woes of other people's issues. This is where the King of Cups excels, as this King is a master of the human condition. He may not be as lively and outgoing as the King of Wands, but he has other strengths the wands lacks. He has emotional depth, loyalty and passion. The King of Cups may at times have the coldness of the King of Swords, but this is because he has retreated into himself. Eventually his warmth comes back out if you give him his space to re-calibrate. The King of Cups is a strong, yet gentle compassionate lover and helper to those who need it.

On the challenging side, the King of Cups can be moody, withdrawn, or even passive aggressive on a bad day, but on a good day he is friendly, alluring, intoxicating, and compassionate. This is a wise teacher who doesn't allow his emotions to fly like fire the way the other Court cards in the Cups suit might, but if he's pushed, then his anger is worse than all of them put together creating a tidal wave that destroys anything in its wake.

SITUATION:

The King of Cups can be asking you to awaken your creative side. It may be to add some feeling to your decision making or it's asking you to operate from the heart. Be compassionate in a situation that requires it. This is also asking you to keep your emotions balanced like this King if you've been running off the track. It is to be the calm within the storm in situations. This can indicate positive work endeavors or love relationships.

In love, this may show a partner coming in who is emotionally stable and emotionally fulfilling. If you had been with passionless partners, or those who didn't seem to care about your feelings, then the King of Cups shows someone who is compassionate and caring coming in.

If you're already in a love relationship, then this can be asking you both to open up with one another about how you're feeling. It could be the couple is emotionally distant, which is not helping in bonding them together. The opposite can confirm this is an emotionally stable and loving couple.

In general, this can be asking you to be a listening ear to others. Pay attention to your own needs and desires. Like all court cards, you are asked to dive into the traits of that court card. With the King of

Cups, that means observing a strong emotional calm in situations you're faced with. In any kind of crises or tense situation, you are asked to remain centered.

Yes, No, Maybe

*T*his section is a cheat sheet guide on what cards can indicate a yes, no, or maybe. These are not hard and true guidelines, but my Spirit team's interpretation of what the response is. In the end, follow your own hunches on what feels right for you with your own team. If you disagree with a card being a yes, no, or maybe, then change it to what you feel the card's response is to you.

When you decide to make a card a different response, then you must keep it that same *yes, no, maybe* response whenever you conduct a reading. One of the reasons is that when you are making a card a particular *yes, no, maybe* response, then you are also making this agreement with your Spirit team as well too. The other reason is that if you continuously change the response to suit what you desire the response to be to a question, then you taint your reading. Both of these reasons can make your reading inaccurate in the end.

The "maybe" response listed in this cheat sheet means there is a 50/50 shot that it can go either way depending on various factors. For example, you're wondering if the guy/girl you have a crush on is the one. You get a "maybe" card. This can mean that yes there is a possibility, but one or the both of you will need to make a move or the answer will be a 'no'. If you both make a move, then the "maybe" can be turned into a 'yes'.

The list of cards under the *yes, no, and maybe* categories are a guide, but not set in stone. Everything in this book is a generalization of potential possibilities and samples of what a card can mean. In the end, you as the reader follow your own guide as to what feels right to you. This is merely a structure for you to jump off of.

0 – The Fool	Maybe	11 – Justice	Yes
1 - The Magician	Yes	12 - The Hanged Man	Maybe
2 - The High Priestess	Yes	13 – Death	No
3 - The Empress	Yes	14 – Temperance	Maybe
4 - The Emperor	Yes	15 - The Devil	No
5 - The Hierophant	Maybe	16 - The Tower	No
6 - The Lovers	Yes	17 - The Star	Yes
7 - The Chariot	Yes	18 - The Moon	Maybe
8 - Strength	Yes	19 - The Sun	Yes
9 - The Hermit	Yes	20 - Judgement	Yes
10 - The Wheel	Yes	21 - The World	Yes

Ace of Wands	Yes	Ace of Swords	Yes
Two of Wands	Maybe	Two of Swords	Maybe
Three of Wands	Yes	Three of Swords	No
Four of Wands	Yes	Four of Swords	Maybe
Five of Wands	No	Five of Swords	No
Six of Wands	Yes	Six of Swords	Maybe
Seven of Wands	Maybe	Seven of Swords	No
Eight of Wands	Yes	Eight of Swords	No
Nine of Wands	Maybe	Nine of Swords	No
Ten of Wands	No	Ten of Swords	No
Page of Wands	Yes	Page of Swords	Yes
Knight of Wands	Yes	Knight of Swords	Yes
Queen of Wands	Yes	Queen of Swords	Maybe
King of Wands	Yes	King of Swords	Maybe

Ace of Pentacles	Yes	Ace of Cups	Yes
Two of Pentacles	Maybe	Two of Cups	Yes
Three of Pentacles	Yes	Three of Cups	Yes
Four of Pentacles	Maybe	Four of Cups	Maybe
Five of Pentacles	No	Five of Cups	No
Six of Pentacles	Yes	Six of Cups	Yes
Seven of Pentacles	Maybe	Seven of Cups	Maybe
Eight of Pentacles	Yes	Eight of Cups	No
Nine of Pentacles	Yes	Nine of Cups	Yes
Ten of Pentacles	Yes	Ten of Cups	Yes
Page of Pentacles	Yes	Page of Cups	Yes
Knight of Pentacles	Yes	Knight of Cups	Yes
Queen of Pentacles	Yes	Queen of Cups	Yes
King of Pentacles	Yes	King of Cups	Yes

The Essential Kevin Hunter Collection
Available in Paperback and E-book

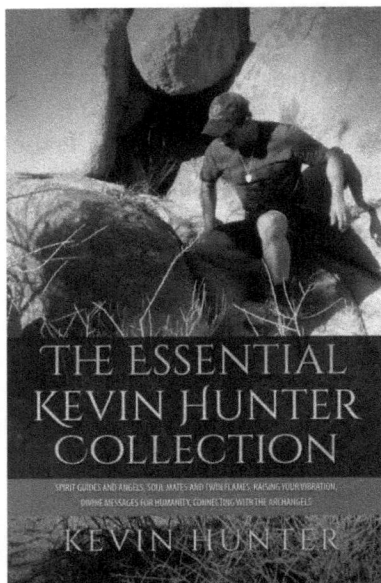

THE ESSENTIAL
KEVIN HUNTER
COLLECTION

Featuring the following books:
Warrior of Light, Empowering Spirit Wisdom, Darkness of Ego,
Spirit Guides and Angels, Soul Mates and Twin Flames, Raising
Your Vibration, Divine Messages for Humanity, and Connecting
with the Archangels.

A Beginner's Guide to the Four Psychic Clair Senses
Clairvoyance, Clairaudience, Claircognizance, Clairsentience

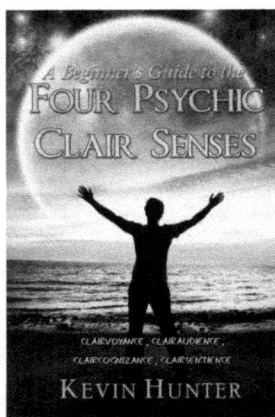

The *Four Psychic Clair Senses* gives examples and
scenarios of what the core etheric senses are in
detail, examples of how the author picks up on
messages, how you can, and other fun spiritual
psychic stuff! Read about the four core clairs in
order to pinpoint what best describes you and
how to have a better understanding of what they
are and how they work for you.

WARRIOR OF LIGHT
Messages from my Guides and Angels

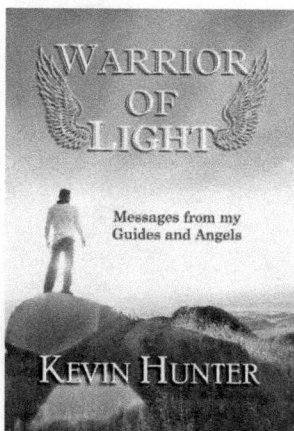

There are legions of angels, spirit guides, and departed loved ones in heaven that watch and guide you on your journey here on Earth. They are around to make your life easier and less stressful. Do you pay attention to the nudges, guidance, and messages given to you? There are many who live lives full of negativity and stress while trying to make ends meet. This can shake your faith as it leads you down paths of addictions, unhealthy life choices, and negative relationship connections. Learn how you can recognize the guidance of your own Spirit team of guides and angels around you.

Author, Kevin Hunter, relays heavenly guided messages about getting humanity, the world, and yourself into shape. He delivers the guidance passed onto him by his own Spirit team on how to fine tune your body, soul and raise your vibration. Doing this can help you gain hope and faith in your own life in order to start attracting in more abundance.

EMPOWERING SPIRIT WISDOM
A Warrior of Light's Guide on Love, Career and the Spirit World

Kevin Hunter relays heavenly, guided messages for everyday life concerns with his book, *Empowering Spirit Wisdom*. Some of the topics covered are your soul, spirit and the power of the light, laws of attraction, finding meaningful work, transforming your professional and personal life, navigating through the various stages of dating and love relationships, as well as other practical affirmations and messages from the Archangels. Kevin Hunter passes on the sensible wisdom given to him by his own Spirit team in this inspirational book.

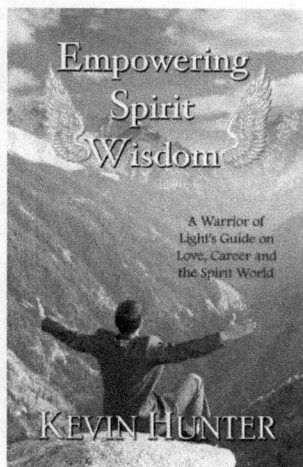

DARKNESS OF EGO

In *Darkness of Ego*, author Kevin Hunter infuses some of the guidance, messages, and wisdom he's received from his Spirit team surrounding all things ego related. The ego is one of the most damaging culprits in human life. Therefore, it is essential to understand the nature of the beast in order to navigate gracefully out of it when it spins out of control. Some of the topics covered in *Darkness of Ego* are humanity's destruction, mass hysteria, karmic debt, and the power of the mind, heaven's gate, the ego's war on love and relationships, and much more.

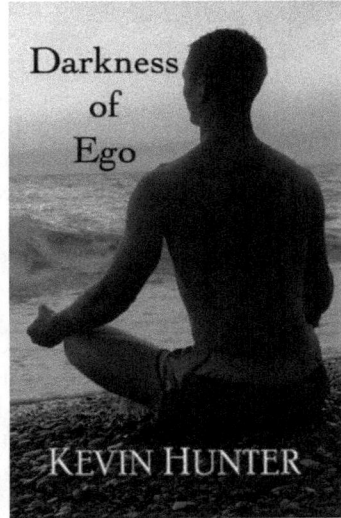

REACHING FOR THE WARRIOR WITHIN

Reaching for the Warrior Within is the author's personal story recounting a volatile childhood. This led him to a path of addictions, anxiety and overindulgence in alcohol, drugs, cigarettes and destructive relationships. As a survival mechanism, he split into many different "selves". He credits turning his life around, not by therapy, but by simultaneously paying attention to the messages he has been receiving from his Spirit team in Heaven since birth.

REALM OF THE WISE ONE

In the Spirit Worlds and the dimensions that exist, reside numerous kingdoms that house a plethora of Spirits that inhabit various forms. One of these tribes is called the Wise Ones, a darker breed in the spirit realm who often chooses to incarnate into a human body one lifetime after another for important purposes.

The *Realm of the Wise One* takes you on a magical journey to the spirit world where the Wise Ones dwell. This is followed with in-depth and detailed information on how to recognize a human soul who has incarnated from the Wise One Realm.

Author, Kevin Hunter, is a Wise One who uses the knowledge passed onto him by his Spirit team of Guides and Angels to relay the wisdom surrounding all things Wise One. He discusses the traits, purposes, gifts, roles, and personalities among other things that make up someone who is a Wise One.

Wise Ones have come in the guises of teachers, shaman, leaders, hunters, mediums, entertainers and others. *Realm of the Wise One* is an informational guide devoted to the tribe of the Wise Ones, both in human form and on the other side.

IGNITE YOUR INNER LIFE FORCE

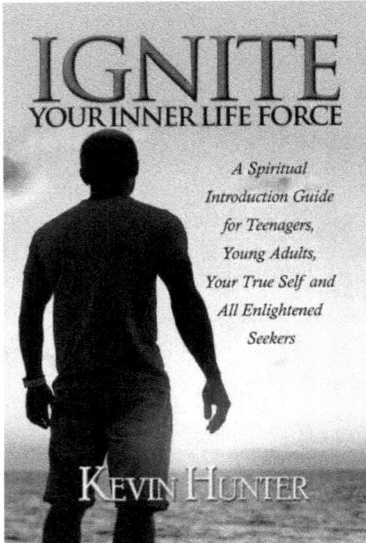

Ignite Your Inner Life Force is an introduction guide for teens, young adults, and anyone seeking answers, messages, and guidance and surrounding spiritual empowerment. This is from understanding what Heaven, the soul, and spiritual beings are to knowing when you are connecting with your Spirit team of Guides and Angels.

Some of the topics covered are communicating with Heaven, working with your Spirit team, what your higher self is, your life purpose and soul contract, what the ego is, love and relationships, your vibration energy, shifting your consciousness and thinking for yourself even when you stand alone. This is an in-depth primer manual offering you foundation as you find a higher purpose navigating through your personal journey in today's modern day practical world.

AWAKEN YOUR CREATIVE SPIRIT

Your creative spirit is more than being artistic and getting involved in creativity pursuits, although this is a good part of it. When your creative spirit is activated by a high vibration state of being, then this is the space you create from. You can apply this to your dealings in life, your creative and artistic pursuits, and to having a greater communication line with your Spirit team on the Other Side. *Awaken Your Creative Spirit* is an overview of what it means to have access to Divine assistance and how that plays a part in arousing the muse within you in order to bring your state of mind into a happier space.

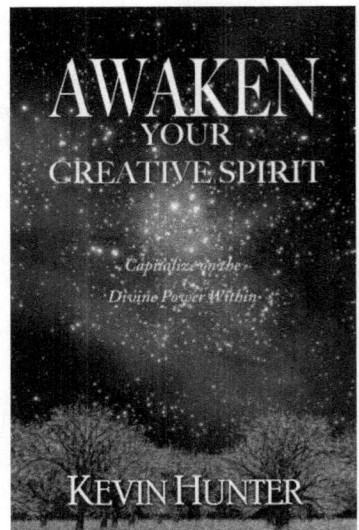

The *Warrior of Light* series of mini-pocket books are available in paperback and E-book by Kevin Hunter called, *Spirit Guides and Angels, Soul Mates and Twin Flames, Divine Messages for Humanity, Raising Your Vibration, Connecting with the Archangels, and The Seven Deadly Sins*

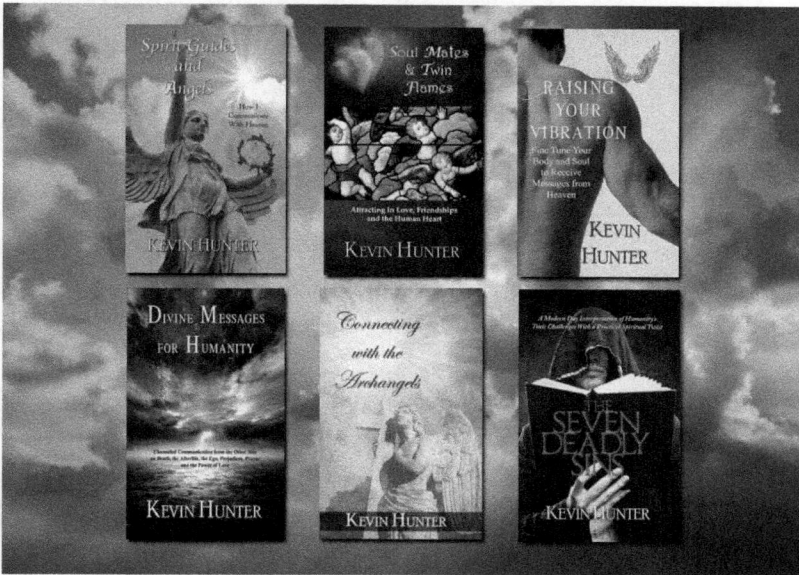

About the Author

Kevin Hunter is an author, love expert, and channeler. His books tackle a variety of genres and tend to have a strong male protagonist. The messages and themes he weaves in his work surround Spirit's own communications of love and respect which he channels and infuses into his writing work.

His spiritually based empowerment books include *Warrior of Light, Empowering Spirit Wisdom, Realm of the Wise One, Reaching for the Warrior Within, Darkness of Ego, Ignite Your Inner Life Force, Awaken Your Creative Spirit, The Seven Deadly Sins, Four Psychic Clair Senses* and *Tarot Card Meanings*. He is also the author of the dating guide *Love Party of One*, the horror/drama, *Paint the Silence*, and the modern day erotic love story, *Jagger's Revolution*.

Before becoming an author, Kevin started out in the entertainment business in 1996 as the personal development guy to one of Hollywood's most respected talent, Michelle Pfeiffer, for her boutique production company, Via Rosa Productions. She dissolved her company after several years and he made a move into coordinating film productions for the big studios on such films as *One Fine Day, A Thousand Acres, The Deep End of the Ocean, Crazy in Alabama, The Perfect Storm, Original Sin, Harry Potter & the Sorcerer's Stone, Dr. Dolittle 2,* and *Carolina*. He considers himself a beach bum born and raised in Southern California. For more information, www.kevin-hunter.com